The
Hamster
HANDBOOK

PATRICIA BARTLETT

BARRON'S

Acknowledgments

There are many people who deserve my sincere thanks for this book. First of all is my husband Dick, who shared my enthusiasm for these creatures, and the ever helpful Linda Price of AAA Hamsters; Anie Hansen; Helen Brinkworth; and Dymph Lappé. I owe a special debt to the hamster keepers who post deails on hamster care and rearing on *Hamster.com* and other hamster websites. Their concern and involvement with the hobby demonstrate to others how to care for these pocket-rodents.

About the Author

Patricia Bartlett is an author who writes about historical and natural history topics. Before turning to writing, she worked as a museum director, a book editor, an Asian studies coordinator, and a magazine production manager. She has written for Web sites, trade publications, newspapers, and popular magazines. She has authored or coauthored some sixty books on history or natural history.

All inquiries should be addressed to:
Barron's Educational Series, Inc.
250 Wireless Boulevard
Hauppauge, New York 11788
www.barronseduc.com

ISBN: 978-1-4380-0489-1

Library of Congress Control No. 2014032794

Library of Congress Cataloging-in-Publication Data
Bartlett, Patricia, 1949–
The hamster handbook/Patricia Bartlett.—2nd edition.
   pages cm.—(Barron's pet handbooks)
Includes index.
ISBN 978-1-4380-0489-1
 1. Hamsters as pets. I. Title.
SF459.H3B38 2015
636.935'6—dc23   2014032794

Printed in China
9 8 7 6 5 4 3 2 1

Cover Photos

Shutterstock:
 Anastasia Solovykh: inside back cover
 Kuttelvaserova Stuchelova: back cover (bottom)
 Stanislaw Sulica: inside front cover
 stock_shot: front cover, back cover (top)
 Vishnevskiy Vasily: spine

Photo Credits

R. D. Bartlett: pages 7, 8, 23, 28, 32, 38, 40, 47, 49 (top and bottom), 51, 52, 76, 82, 91, 94, 95, 116, 117, 119
fotolia: Krzysztof Bajor: page 27
Anie Hansen: pages 10, 19, 43, 48 (top and bottom)
iStock: abalcazar: page 37
Zig Leszc: pages 2, 4, 46 (top), 58, 59, 62, 65, 67, 69, 80, 84, 85, 107
Popular Science magazine: page 12
Quality Cage Company: page 36
Shutterstock: ADA_photo: page 114; Africa Studio: page 102; AlexBukharov: page 18; AlexKalashnikov: page 68; Alexruss: page 6; Anastasia Solovykh: page 20, 112; Andy Lidstone: page 66; Antonio Martin: page 103; Artem and Olga Sapegin: pages 41, 42; Attasuntorn Traisuwan: page 88; bioraven: page 56; cath5: page 45; Charles Edwards: page 29; cynoclub: page 98; Denisa Doudova: page 55; dwori: page 70; Ekaterina Pokrovskaya: page 79; Elya Vatel: page 5; Emilia Stasiak: pages 30, 33, 104; Eric Isselee: page 74; gulserinak1955: page 14; Hintau Aliaksei: page 21; Jagodka: page 101; Julia Kuznetsova: page 108; Lasse Kristensen: page 60; Lepas: page 93; Maros Bauer: page 25; Ostanina Ekaterina: page 73; Sandy Schulze: page 13; Sethislav: page 111; Smit: page 16; Steve Design: pages 71, 90; stock_shot: pages 15, 31, 96, 120, 122; Subbotina Anna: page 34; Tateos: page 50; VeryOlive: page 87; Victoria Rak: page 46 (bottom); Vishnevskiy Vasily: page 26, 39; Ziolkowski Dariusz: page 113
Martina Umlauft: pages 9, 100

Contents

Introduction

Long Ago and Far Away

Actually, the "long ago" equates to somewhat more than sixty five years ago, and the "far away" land was my boyhood home in western Massachusetts. As I sit typing in my north-central Florida office, the Connecticut River valley is pretty much a faraway land. But a little hamster, re-arranging the bedding in her cage next to my desk, brings back some memories.

Even as a lad I was enamored of all manner of animals, and fortunately, my parents indulged my interests. The nightly reading of the "Pets for Sale" ads in the local newspaper was pretty much a ritual. One night, while reading the usual ads for dogs and cats, I recall my father stopping and asking, "What's a hamster?" I was all of ten years old and certainly had no idea. My father read the ad to me. "Syrian golden hamsters, $10 each," and then added a phone number. "Let's call," he said.

So we did and were told that a golden hamster was like a little teddy bear. My father asked the seller if he'd take anything less than $10 (after all, $10 was a lot of money in 1948). After a little dickering, a price of $16 for a pair was agreed upon, and we went to see what a golden hamster really was.

The seller was across town, so of course we tried to figure out during the drive what it was we were actually going to see. I guess we came up with something, but it certainly wasn't at all like the little creatures we ultimately saw.

When we arrived, the seller took us down into his cellar, and there in a half-dozen 10-gallon terraria were a couple dozen baby golden hamsters. Although they didn't look much like bears to me, it was love at first sight. I knew that my allowance, both saved and for the foreseeable future, was going to be spent that day. And when we left, half an hour later, we had a cardboard box that contained a pair of young golden hamsters.

That pair of hamsters thrived and bred like the rodents they were. Only a matter of weeks after I got them, they had bred and produced their first litter of babies. A few weeks later those babies begat babies of their own, and soon all my neighborhood friends had baby hamsters. We put our own ads in the paper and were able to sell a few— but only at reduced prices. Some went to pet stores, some to other breeders. Eventually all I had left was my original pair. And after a time they were too old

A hamster wakes up.

to breed. Although I can't remember for certain, I imagine that my entire family breathed a sigh of relief.

But I do remember that from nearly complete obscurity, Syrian golden hamsters became a veritable pet rage. The little critters were in every pet store, as well as in the pet sections of what were then called five-and-dime stores, which were sort of tiny Walmarts. I thought it phenomenal that a little rodent—a member of a group not particularly liked by people—could become so popular.

A dozen years later, golden hamsters still held pet appeal. I then was managing a pet distribution company in central Florida, and our hamster sales stood at about two thousand of the animals weekly. This was when hamsters of "odd" colors were making their debut. We were able to offer a fair percentage of the unusual banded hamsters, which were snapped up by our customers.

I still find hamsters among the most endearing of rodents, and as they wander from place to place, cheek pouches full to overflowing with seeds and fruits, they remind me of Mr. Magoo, the myopic bumbling cartoon character who always seems to come out on top. How could one not fall for such an enchanting creature?

Dick Bartlett

Preface
(A Word for Parents)

Acquiring a hamster may be part of a purposeful act, or it may just "happen." Hamsters certainly have all the points when it comes to being cute, small, and furry, and they can be hard to resist. When you realize that their basic care isn't all that complex or expensive, the temptation grows.

For many people, owning a hamster is part of being a parent, and part of helping a child learn responsibility. The first decision is not "What kind of hamster do we want?" but rather "Who is going to take on which part of this creature's care?" Sometimes kids are just too young to regularly deal with set tasks. Once everyone agrees on which responsibilities belong where, you can proceed to the best way to acquire the new pet.

One way or another, either through your children's friends, a neighbor, or a school project, a cage with a hamster appears on the kitchen table, rather like a conjuror's trick. You regard the cage with faint surprise and a little bit of suspicion. "Was I part of this decision?" you ask, although no one answers. "Was I awake at the time?" There's still no answer, nor do you expect one. You already know that hamsters are legendary for their prowess in reproduction, and you're not fooled for a moment that the hamster in the cage before you has been in solitary confinement all its life, even if your child assures you it's a male and could not possibly be pregnant. You rather expect to wake up early some morning to your kid's delighted squeal, "Fred had babies! Look!" What you may not expect is a litter size of twelve.

This book is designed to take some of the work out of hamster keeping and to make the process enjoyable. Hamsters are far more than short-tailed mice wannabes. Hamsters are actually a group of about two dozen related species, all lumped together under the term "hamster," like all dogs are lumped into the "dog" group. Some types have a well-developed social environment, living cheerfully together in underground warrens they excavate themselves, and even live with other species. ("A pika! C'mon in! There's plenty of room!") Others want absolute solitude except for brief sexual contacts.

Hamsters are by nature wanderers. If necessary, the Syrian hamster (once called the golden hamster) may travel far from its burrow each night in search of food. As it travels, the hamster will shove seeds and other bits of vegetation into his capacious cheek pouches.

A classic banded Syrian hamster.

Once back in his sleeping area, he'll use his front feet to help empty the pouches, shoving the contents busily from behind with much the same distracted "I'm late!" attitude of the March hare, before heading out again. Whether a hamster is from the wild or from the Bronx, once dawn breaks over the horizon, it's bedtime and the hamster is horizontal and gently snoozing.

The dining habits of hamsters have pretty much made them the enemy of farmers in their native homelands. They can become extremely numerous over part of their range. (A gestation period of 16–20 days and a litter size of 4–14 young play a role in this.) Working quietly at night, hamsters mow down swaths of wheat, oats, or other grain crops, neatly severing the stems at the ground and then nipping the stems into portable or pouchable lengths. The communal types may stash away up to 240 pounds (90 kgs) of grains, grasses, legumes, insect larvae, and potatoes in their community larder. You can understand why a farmer wouldn't welcome their presence. Provide a small area for hoarding in your hamster's cage; as long as he doesn't tuck away food items that will spoil (or as long as you take those bits out), he'll seem more secure.

The nocturnal habits of hamsters mean they are totally okay with being left alone during the day. When you get home in the afternoon or evening and have a bit of time, your pet is ready to wake up and enjoy your attention.

Unlike rats or mice, hamsters have no detectable body odor—at least, not detectable to humans, which makes holding one, playing with one, pretending you've lost one as he scurries between your bedsheets, or offering your new pet a sunflower seed treat, more enjoyable. Because their urine is far less pungent than that of other rodents, cage cleaning is less onerous. With an adult weight of 4–6 ounces, keeping your hamster well fed won't be an expensive proposition. Each eats between 1 to 2 tablespoons of feed a day, every day.

Chapter One
The Hamster's Past

The laurel wreath for hamsters as pets can be proudly claimed by three men—by Saul Adler, an English parasitologist; by Israel Aharoni, a zoologist from the University of Jerusalem; and by Albert Marsh, a highway engineer from Mobile, Alabama.

All of these men recognized the pet potential of the Syrian or golden hamster. Saul Adler gets the credit for realizing there *had* to be hamsters from the wild he could use in his research, and for sharing those hamsters once he got them; Aharoni gets the credit for his friendship with Adler and his dogged determination to literally dig out those first hamsters and (with the help of his wife) raise their young. Marsh gets the credit for starting a hamstery and for quite probably starting one of the first, if not *the* first, "make money by raising these animals at home" operations.

But let's start at the beginning, and for the beginning of the hamster we need to go to the 1700s, because like everything else, history has a way of creeping into any discussion you have about any animal. For all of us, the domesticated hamster begins with the Syrian or golden hamster, *Mesocricetus auratus* (meaning "almost like but not quite Cricetus" [the European hamster] and "golden," for its golden brown color).

The earliest published description or reference to the Syrian golden hamster was in the second edition of a book titled *The Natural History of Aleppo*. In 1740, an English physician named Alexander Russell was practicing in Aleppo, Syria, a country that in those days was beyond the ends of the earth. (Syria lies along the easternmost end of the Mediterranean Sea, just west of the island of Cyprus and south of Turkey. It is no longer a faraway country but has been front and center in world attention because it has been torn apart by civil war and violence since the 1980s.)

Alexander Russell was the physician for an English trading company in Aleppo and became a favored physician of the local pasha. In keeping with what a learned man would do in a new land, Alexander Russell took notes on the people, local flora and fauna, and the plague. He became a bit of an expert on the plague, but there are no indications anywhere that he knew of the correlation between rodents and the spread of the plague. (Scientific analysis was a new approach, back then. A concept as basic as asepsis, or cleanliness, wouldn't be proposed in England until 1865.) In his spare time, Russell

It is in the second edition that the golden hamster first appeared. Alexander may have known about the animal, but it was Patrick who first published the account. Patrick Russell wasn't all that wordy, his account is limited to a paragraph that described the number of French beans the animal had stuffed in parallel rows into its cheek pouches. Obviously, he was working with a hamster corpse. Russell commented about the green beans: "When they were laid loosely on the table, they formed a heap three times the bulk of the animal's body." Hamsters deserve their reputation for being able to carry a lot of food.

Patrick Russell thought the animal was essentially the same animal as the European hamster and referenced it *Mus cricetus*, or the Mouse Golden. He did not record what he did with that animal. But like his brother, he deserves to be recognized as a science-minded man, careful in his observations and his writing.

And there the information on the hamster remained, until 1839. That year, George Waterhouse, the curator of the London Zoological Society, made a presentation at a meeting of the Society and described a new species of hamster. He based his description on the preserved skin and skull from a single specimen, which the Society had received from Aleppo. He named it *Cricetus auretus*, or Golden hamster. The collector of the animal was unknown (but it would be hard to point the finger at anyone other than Patrick Rus-

Saul Adler's difficulty in getting the Chinese hamster (like the one shown here) led to the capture of the Syrian hamster.

put together a book and called it *The Natural History of Aleppo*. He published it in 1756, after he had left Syria.

Alexander's younger brother, Patrick, lived in Aleppo from 1750 to 1781. He made further notes and published the second edition of the natural history in 1797, after the death of his elder brother. (Both editions are long out of print. Once in a while, the first edition, the hamsterless one, is available from used-book dealers, for about $1600. There are reprints available for about $30.)

sell). Some years later the genus was changed to *Mesocricetus.*

It would seem that the announcement of a new species of hamster would have excited someone (after all, they didn't even have electricity or lightbulbs back in 1839), but indeed, the Syrian hamster, having had its brief brush with fame, sank again into obscurity until the late 1920s or perhaps even early 1930.

Enter Saul Adler. Adler was a parasitologist at the Hebrew University of Jerusalem. He was using the Chinese hamster to study a disease called leishmaniasis (also called kala-azar), which is caused by a protozoan-like parasite that is spread by the bite of a sandfly. The Chinese hamster (*Cricetulus griseus*, a variation of Cricetus and gray) had proven to be a good study animal for the disease, but Adler was running into a wall. He was unable to breed enough of them for his research, not knowing about the importance of long days and short days for the reproduction of this small-sized hamster, and shipments of additional hamsters from China were unreliable. (China, as a country, had huge troubles of its own at the time. A new national government had come into power in 1929, only to be smacked with two widespread rebellions. The country was also in the middle of a famine that had killed some three million people. In addition, the world at large was in the depths of a disastrous financial crisis called the Great Depression.)

Adler needed a hamster species that would be easy to obtain. He asked a colleague who was frequently in the field to find and bring back hamsters, for his research. What could be easier?

The colleague was Israel Aharoni. In addition to being a zoologist, Aharoni was a linguist, speaking and reading Arabic, Latin, Greek, Aramaic, and other European languages, as well as Hebrew. One of Aharoni's projects was to research the Hebrew names for the animals of the Holy Land and produce a record of what animals had actually lived there. Because Aharoni collected butterflies (he was a zoologist, remem-

Hunted almost to extinction, the wild European hamster is now protected. Today a few fur farms in Europe raise this hamster for its distinctive coat.

ber?), he had become firm friends with a Turkish sultan who also collected butterflies. At the time, that part of the Middle East was under Turkish rule.

In 1930, Aharoni went into the field to look for hamsters for Adler. But he wasn't just casting around blindly; he was pretty sure where to look.

When he got to the Aleppo area, he instructed his guide to entreat the local sheik for information about the location of what was then called the golden hamster. The sheik was amenable and sent Aharoni and his crew to a cultivated field that indeed had a population of hamsters. The sheik even provided laborers to dig up the hamsters, to the dismay of the farmer, who watched the hole in his grain field get bigger and bigger. From an excavation 8 feet deep, the crew dug up a nest of a mother and eleven young.

The mother and litter were placed together in a box. Perhaps the collectors stood over the box congratulating themselves and each other but then saw what happened next. You may already know exactly what happened if you know what a highly stressed hamster can do if she and her young are disturbed. The mother hamster killed the first pup that approached her after they were placed in the box.

The collectors were shocked, and the mother was removed and killed. Aharoni (and his wife) took on the task of raising the remaining ten pups. We don't know, of course, how old the pups were, only that their eyes were still closed. But Syrian babies nibble on solid food shortly after they first begin exploring out of the nest at nine to ten days, eyes still closed, so perhaps the babies were easy for the Aharonis to feed.

Aharoni had great intentions, but admittedly he and his forbearing wife were neophytes at hamster-raising. The pups were placed in a wooden cage, and the growing hamsters soon figured out how to gnaw their way to freedom. They escaped twice from their caging, and not all of them were recaptured (hamsters are escape artists—remember this).

Vienna is a Golden dominant spot Syrian.

Only four reached breeding age, and after an unfortunate mishap during a breeding effort, only three were left. Fortunately, both sexes were represented. A pair was placed in a hay-packed cage, and the hamsters did exactly what they were supposed to do, which was mate and *not* kill each other (it was just a quirk that they were placed together during the correct time in the female's cycle, when she was receptive).

Aharoni greeted the birth of that first litter as if they were the only hamsters in the universe. His notes include a little prophecy, which is so flowery one can't help but wonder if some libation was involved.

> "Only someone who has tasted true happiness, heavenly joy, can appreciate our elation over the fact that our efforts did not prove in vain . . . From now on there will be a species of hamster that will be fruitful and multiply even in captivity, and will be convenient for laboratory experimentation. How marvelous are thy works, O Lord!"

The offspring of that first union were raised successfully. They mated, and their young grew up and mated, etc., until the colony numbered 150. This took less than a year. (There's another lesson here.)

Aharoni sent the colony to Adler, and Adler was able to continue his research. He published his work with the Syrian hamsters in 1931. A generous man, he then provided breeding stock to other laboratories, including those in England.

There is no official date for this transfer, because it wasn't an official action: the British stock was brought in, quietly, in Adler's pockets.

As time went on, Adler continued his extraordinary work on leishmaniasis and evolution, and translated Darwin's *Origin of Species* into Hebrew. But he always took particular pride in his role in bringing the Syrian hamster to science.

Hamsters Gain a Foothold in the United States

Adler knew how quickly a research colony of any animal can succumb to an unknown malady. He continued his sharing, this time with a research facility in India before the Second World War. His contact there sent hamsters to the United States, to Case Western Reserve School of Medicine in Cleveland (OH), and the Rockefeller Foundation in New York. An even dozen hamsters were sent to the Public Health Service in Carville, Louisiana.

There was a reason why Carville was singled out. Carville was the site of the only leprosarium in the United States. Leprosy was considered such a disfiguring, communicable, and incurable disease in those days that those who contracted it were quarantined for life in leprosariums (you can read some of the 1938 issues of the *International Journal of Leprosy* online for a look at the seriousness of this disease). Science

was unable to find a cure for leprosy because there didn't seem to be an animal other than humans that could contract the disease. Obviously, research opportunities were limited.

With the thought that maybe the Syrian hamsters could be that longed-for research animal, hamsters were sent to Carville. Alas, the hamsters were as resistant as all other animals thus far to leprosy (it wasn't until the 1980s that scientists found that armadillos could contract leprosy, but they'd already found ways to absolutely cure the disease in the 1940s, so the armadillos that wander the South are safe).

Carville's hamsters arrived in July of 1938, and a year later, Dr. S. H. Black of the laboratory dutifully reported in what was then the *Journal of Leprosy* his success on breeding the Syrian hamster (by this time, surely everyone connected to Syrian breeding projects had figured out that Syrians have a gestation period of about 16 days).

Of course those first three institutions shared their hamsters with other labs ("Here! Take a dozen! Take three

dozen! But hurry!"). Hamsters were sent to a lab in Berkeley, California, the NIH labs, and Tumblebrook Farms in Massachusetts (Tumblebrook was already a supplier of line-bred mice to research facilities). Twelve hamsters were sent to Washington University in St. Louis, Missouri. Every resource agreed the Syrian hamster was the dreamed-for research animal. And, that viewpoint hasn't changed much over the years.

Enter Albert Marsh, of Mobile, Alabama. Marsh was a highway engineer, a bit of a visionary, and a bit of a carny. He won a Syrian hamster in a bet. Intrigued with the little animal, he acquired more, somehow (Carville is the closest, most logical source, but no one knows for sure. Any transfer could easily have been, ah, informal), and set up his own colony. He named his business the Gulf Hamstery and Marsh Enterprises and went to work breeding hamsters and promoting them as pets.

Marsh had a flair for the business, and he certainly knew how to work hard. He sold hamsters to individuals. He sold to laboratories. He took out ads in farming journals and *Popular Science* magazine and promised to buy every hamster the reader could produce ("$1.00 for females and 75 cents for males at weaning age," which was real money in 1948). He served as an intermediary, buying hamsters from breeders and having them drop-shipped directly to other customers. He wrote a book on raising and breeding hamsters, and published it himself. His photograph in the book shows him with hamsters in each hand and crawling out of the pockets of his long-sleeved white shirt; one hopes the photo was posed.

By 1951, Marsh's book had sold so well it was in its sixth edition, and there were a lot of hamsters in the pet market. By 1953, a "Success at Home" article in the Springfield, Massachusetts, *Union* newspaper estimated Marsh's weekly gross income at $4,000.

Marsh even found time to do a little political maneuvering to increase his market share of a booming business. In 1948, hamsters could not be brought into the state of California, because they were considered a "wild animal." Marsh, with the help of the governor of Alabama, got California to recognize Syrian hamsters as domestic animals, thereby opening a new market for his enterprise. One can't help but wonder why the governor of Alabama would get involved with a rodent-breeding operation, but maybe by then there were a LOT of hamsters in Alabama.

But as with any new product, the laws of supply and demand caught up with Marsh. Pet stores began to buy their hamsters from inexpensive local backyard breeders.

Infectious enteritis (called "wet-tail" because of the unending and deadly diarrhea that is spread by hamster-to-hamster contact or by contaminated hands or bedding) made hamsters

The pet market depends on "new" Syrians with different colors and coat textures. This one is a male Syrian longhair.

A hamster stands just inside the door to see if an intruder is friendly or not.

unprofitable for many pet stores (antibiotic use for lab animals or pets was still in the future).

Marsh's markets dried up, and so did his hamstery. He moved to California and began breeding quail commercially. But thanks to his work and his ability to hustle, hamsters had found an unbeatable niche in the pet market, and the pet industry had helped solidify that niche by developing and marketing caging, foods, and accessories.

Today, the numbers of hamsters bred and used for research far outnumber those in the pet market. Laboratories buy hamsters from large commercial breeding facilities with well-documented lineages and rigid breeding standards. In 2010, the USDA reported some 64,000 hamsters were used in research in the United States alone. Ninety percent of those were Syrians.

But the saga of the "wild" Syrian hamster doesn't end with the 1930 imports.

In 1971, Michael R. Murphy, then a graduate student at Massachusetts Institute of Technology, went to Aleppo, Syria, for the express purpose of capturing wild Syrian hamsters and bringing them back for comparative research; after all, up to that point every single Syrian hamster in the lab and pet markets was a descendant of that single pair from 1930.

Murphy and his wife, Janet, captured and brought back a dozen hamsters, and in the process, the hamster's charm hit again. Murphy commented that after only three days of handling, the hamsters he captured were tame and gentle. Those hamsters bred within a month of being captured, and all eight young were brought up to weaning (the lessons learned by Aharoni and others have not gone unrefined). In his notes, Murphy added, with gentle understatement, that it looked as if Aharoni was right when he predicted the Syrian hamster would be a wonderful lab animal.

Murphy included a photo in his report. It shows him in the field in Aleppo,

gingerly holding aloft the first wild hamster captured in forty years.

Murphy is, quite understandably, smiling.

Hamster Rumps

It's easy to believe that hamsters have been "the best-ever" small pet for a long time—what's really amazing is the ways people find to enjoy their pets. In Japan, a fad named *hamuketsu* has united gen Y hamster keepers and admirers who jokingly claim hamster bottoms are "so cute you could faint." The name for the fad melds "hamster" with the term for rump, and close-up photos of hamsters, taken from the back, focus attention on plump hamster bottoms. The fad has spawned at least two books featuring hamster rumps.

A hamster fad in Japan centers on photos of hamster rumps.

Chapter Two
The Basic Hamster

The term "hamster" actually refers to about twenty species of small rodents, all from the Old World and all of whom like to hoard food. Hamsters are part of a subfamily of rodents that includes the cotton and wood rats, harvest mice, lemmings, voles, and gerbils. In this subfamily, there are species that climb agilely (harvest mice), species that are excellent swimmers (muskrats), and species that scamper quickly from place to place, usually under cover of darkness (gerbils). Hamsters stand out in the group as secretive burrowers and hoarders. The name "hamster" is said to be derived from the Middle High German *hamastra*, which means to store, referring of course to its habit of storing foodstuffs in its bedding.

The Adaptive Hamster

As a group, hamsters are chunky-bodied, thick-furred, short-tailed rodents with large cheek pouches. They have short limbs, and although there's no opposing thumb on the forefeet, hamsters are quite dexterous when it comes to manipulating food or cage doors. Their teeth have a gap, called the diastema, between the front incisors and the molars. This gap permits the tongue to manipulate food and bedding materials for easy carrying. Some rodents can close their lips behind the incisors, which is why muskrats can gnaw while underwater and naked mole rats can literally chew their way through dirt when digging.

Although hamsters will grab and consume insects such as grasshoppers and mealworms, these dietary items are the exception rather than the rule. The hamster's digestive process and feeding behaviors are those of an herbivore, specialized to deal with a diet that is largely cellulose. Cellulose is hard to break down. This is why cows have more than one stomach and chew their food twice and why termites carry what you might call "digestive" protozoans in their guts (remove the protozoans, and the termites die).

Hamsters digest their own food twice, and a two-compartmented stomach is part of the arrangement. Hamsters are pregastric fermenters, just like the hippopotamus and the kangaroo. This term means that the food is allowed to soften a bit in the first stomach, via fermentation, to aid in the digestive process. (Pregastric fermenters are famous for their gastric

	Syrian Hamster *Mesocricetus auratus*	Campbell's Hamster *Phodophus campbelli*	Winter White Hamster *Phodophus sungorus*	Roborovski Hamster *Phodophus roborovski*	Chinese or Gray Hamster *Cricetus griseus*
Adult length	6–8 inches (15–20 cm)	4–5 inches (10–12 cm)	3–4 inches (8–10 cm)	1.5–2 inches (4–5 cm)	4–5 inches (10–12 cm)
Adult weight	5–7 ounces (140–200 gms)	1.5–2 ounces (40–60 gms)	1.5–2 ounces (40–60 gms)	1–1.5 ounces (25–40 gms)	1.5–1.8 ounces (40– 50 gms)
Adult food consumption	1/3–½ ounce (10–15 gms) dry food/day	¼–½ ounce (7–15 gms) dry food/day	¼–½ ounce (7–15 gms) dry food/day	¼–2/5 ounce (7–12 gms) dry food/day	¼–½ ounce (7–15 gms) dry food/day
Adult water consumption	6 t (30 ml) per day	2–2½–3 t (12–15 ml) per day	2–2½–3 t (12–15 ml) per day	2–2½ t (10–12 ml) per day	2–2½–3 t (12–15 ml) per day

capacity, another reason farmers dislike the wild hamster.)

Food nibbled by the hamster passes through the esophagus to the first compartment of the stomach, called the forestomach. The forestomach is nonglandular, and it serves as sort of a holding bin for the action within. Bacteria in the forestomach begin the digestion process for their hamster host. The process is rather like what happens in the rumen of a cow. It's easy to understand why many antibiotics are deadly to hamsters; they destroy the friendly bacteria in the forestomach but not the pathogenic bacteria. The "bad" bacteria proliferate, with deadly results. But for the hamster we're describing here, everything works just as it should and the semi-fermented food is sloshed through

This rust-colored Syrian will weigh three times a Campbell's weight at maturity.

the stricture into the second section, the glandular stomach, in ten to sixty minutes. Hamsters are efficient when it comes to digestion.

The second "bin" of the stomach is geared up for action with digestive acids to dismantle the food particles. Once the food particles are broken into

absorbable components, they pass into the gut for absorption and extraction/absorption of water. Then the almost-used-up food particles are excreted as soft feces.

Hamsters consume these soft feces, called cecotrophs, as the feces emerge from the anus. The digestion process wrests more nutrition (and a few extra vitamins, including vitamin K) from the cecotrophs, which are then passed from the anus as small, firm feces. The practice is called coprophagy, and hamsters do it up to twenty times a day. Animals that can survive in poor habitat, such as deserts, find ways to gain the most possible out of what they eat and drink, and hamsters are no exception. This ability to wrest vitamin K, which assists in blood clotting, from the diet may be part of the reason that hamsters are naturally resistant to warfarin. Warfarin disables blood-clotting mechanisms and is used for rodent control.

The Hamster Quintet

Of the many kinds of hamsters, only about five are found in the pet marketplace.

The hamster that occupies the front-and-center seat in the pet market is the Syrian hamster, *Mesocricetus auratus*, the "big" hamster (there are bigger hamsters from Middle Europe and Russia, but they aren't in the pet market). Because it was the first pet

hamster and turned out to be incredibly adaptive to captivity, it is the best known of the hamsters. When most people think of hamsters, it's the Syrian that comes to mind.

Three of the other pet hamsters are called the dwarf hamsters, because of their much smaller size—these are the Campbell's, the winter white, and the Roborovski hamsters. They all belong to the genus *Podophus*, and for a while were lumped together in a single genus. You may see them listed with "dwarf" added to their name, as in dwarf Campbell's or dwarf winter white.

The final pet species (and the last to come into the pet market) is the Chinese or gray hamster, *Cricetulus griseus*.

Nico the hamster might resent being called chunky with big cheek pouches—but it's true.

A Syrian hamster learns about its world through scent.

Syrian Origins

Syrian hamsters are found from Rumania and Bulgaria, southeastward to Asia Minor, the Caucasus, Israel, and part of Iran. They are burrowers, living on brushy slopes and steppes, where they dig their own burrows with their feet and teeth or find one to occupy. Burrows can be anywhere from 2 to 10 feet deep, usually with several entrances. Their color is golden brown above, with a creamy white belly and chest. Some have a gray stripe across the chest.

In the wild, Syrians can hibernate in response to cold and/or decreased food supply. Like marmots, they awaken periodically to eat, which is when they nibble on stored food. Researchers A. Terada and N. Ibuka found that older Syrians (20 months old!) start their hibernation earlier and spend more time in the sleeping mode than very young (3 weeks at the start of hibernation) hamsters.

Syrians generally live as individuals in the wild, although families—mother, father, and young—live together until the young reach sexual maturity. Like the European hamsters, each Syrian burrow has its own surrounding territory. They often store food in a communal burrow.

Physical characteristics: At first the Syrian hamster was called the golden hamster, because it was indeed a golden brown color on the top and a pale muddy gray on its stomach (some forms had an ashy stripe across the chest). Because Syrians have now been selectively bred for different colors, one of which is indeed a light

The Pet Hamster Species		
Class	Mammalia, all mammals	
Order	Rodentia, all rodents	
Family	*Muridae*, "mouselike ones," all mice, rats, gerbils, and hamsters	
Subfamily	*Cricetidae*, "squeaking ones," all hamsters	
Genera	*Mesocricetus*, "resembling but not quite like Cricetus," the European field hamster *Phodophus*, "blistered or tubercled foot" *Cricetulus*, "squeaking"	

gold, sometimes the color or pattern is used in its name instead of "Syrian," as in a banded Syrian being sold as a "panda bear hamster." Syrians can be a banded, spotted, solid light gold, black, or any of some twenty-odd colors. Those bright eyes may be black, brown, or a shade of red, and the coat may be long or short. There's even a hairless mutant Syrian called the alien hamster, but they aren't as readily available as the furred type (and not as appealing, either).

Syrians are good-sized rodents, with a body length of 6–8 inches (12–20 cm) and a tail about half an inch long or 12 mm. Adults weigh between 5–7 ounces (140–200 grams). Females are the larger sex. Because Syrians are big, they are easier to handle. Syrians seem to work well for children's pets because of their size, and they don't seem as nervous as the smaller or dwarf hamster types. They respond well to gentle handling and seem to enjoy it.

These are the hamsters with the very large cheek pouches; a fully loaded Syrian looks as if it is wearing a large fur collar. The pouches are very practical ways to carry large amounts of food back to the home area. When the pouches are loaded, the hamster tends to sway a bit from side to side from the added weight. Once they are back in the home burrow, they empty

If given the opportunity, the male Campbell's takes an active role in parenting.

Pet Trade Hamsters at a Glance					
Species	Syrian	Russian	Campbell's	Winter White	Chinese
Size small 2.25–3.75 in.		✗	✗	✗	✗
Size large 3.5–5 in.	✗				
Tail less than 1/3 head–body length	✗	✗	✗	✗	
Tail more than 1/3 body length					✗
Color golden orange or variable	✗				
Color gray or variable			✗	✗	
Color gray		✗			✗
No or poorly defined mid-dorsal stripe	✗	✗			
Well-defined mid-dorsal stripe			✗	✗	✗
Lateral/side stripe present				✗	

the pouches, using their front feet to help shove the food out from behind.

The cheek pouches for Syrians are rather like security blankets. It's always good to have a bit of food at hand, or rather, in cheek, if you're a Syrian. A threatened hamster may empty his cheek pouches if he thinks he may need to run.

Captive life span is 2–2.5 years, but some have lived as long as four years. When you consider the rapid metabolic rate of these creatures–76 breaths a minute, heart rate of 250–500 beats per minute—it becomes easier to understand why the typical life span is twenty-four months.

In captivity, Syrians can have young every month of the year, although there is a marked decrease in fertility during the winter months and after they are over a year and a half old (note: fertility is "greatly reduced" not "ended"). Litter size is usually four to twelve pups, after a gestation of fifteen to eighteen days.

The young begin nibbling at solid food when they're about ten days old and are weaned at three weeks. The young become sexually mature at forty-two days for the males and thirty-four days for the females. Once beyond those dates of sexual maturity, Syrians need to be separated from each other. If they are different sexes, they'll fight and mate, or if they are the same sex, they'll fight. You may have two young Syrians that get along just fine, but fighting is in your future. This usually becomes obvious late at night, when the sounds of tussling and shrill squeaks will resound until you rise up from what had been a deep sleep and roar, "Enough!," rather like Godzilla erupting indignantly out of the ocean after too many sonic-wave tests. Spare your sleep and the health of your hamsters. Separate housing is the only answer.

Lines of inbred Syrian hamsters (20 or more successive generations of brother-sister pairings), or strains, are used for specialized research. Strains are identified by names such as LSH/SsLak. The first three letters identify the lab that developed the strain, in this case the London School of Hygiene.

About the Campbell's Hamster

The second most popular hamster is the dwarf Campbell's Russian hamster, *Phodophus campbelli.* The Campbell's is named for W. C. Campbell who discovered it in Mongolia in 1902. It is found in arid areas in central Asia, northern Russia, Mongolia, and northern China. For a number of years, the Campbell's and the winter whites shared the scientific name *Phodophus sungorus*; they look superficially the same for at least part of the year, and their ranges overlap. They were differentiated on the basis of gut microflora and behavior. You may find the Campbell's listed simply as a "dwarf hamster" in pet stores, or the store may metaphorically toss in the towel and list the Campbell's, the winter white, and the Roborovski hamsters as *Phodophus* sp., which is sort of shorthand for "too hard for us to figure out."

Campbell's hamsters arrived in Britain as lab animals in 1964. They progressed from the lab to the

A platinum red-eyed Campbell's seems far removed from the original brown gray of the original Campbell's.

pet store in the early 1970s and to the United States shortly thereafter. Selective breeding has altered their original coloration—gray-brown with a white belly and a thin, dark mid-dorsal stripe—to some forty color and coat combinations.

When this species was observed in Manchuria in the late 1930s, it was living with pikas and shared the pikas' burrows, paths, and tunnels, especially in the winter. Those observed in the wild dig escape and ventilation tunnels leading away from the burrow entrance. They eat grasses and other vegetation as well as grasshoppers and other insects for moisture and food value. They are efficient at concentrating their urine to conserve water. The females dig a special nesting chamber just before they give birth, and line it with whatever is cozy and available (dried grasses and sheep's wool were typical choices).

In the wild, Campbell's hamsters awaken before dark. They mark their trail with scents from glands behind the ears, on the lower abdomen, and from feces, urine, and (in females) vaginal secretions. Before leaving the area of their burrow, they pause and groom themselves, rubbing their paws over their ears, around the eyes, and by rolling on the ground. This helps transfer the scent to the paws so a scent trail is easily left.

Because they are active for more hours a day, the Campbell's travel farther away from their burrows than their close relative, the winter white hamster. Male Campbell's travel faster than the females, and because of this, they cover a much larger territory over the same amount of time.

The prolonged crepuscular and nighttime activity of the Campbell's indicates that they need more effort and energy to live in their colder, drier, and more seasonal habitat than the winter whites. The extra effort required for survival may also be the reason that both Campbell's parents are involved in care of the young.

Physical characteristics: These are smaller hamsters, weighing about an ounce (females) to two ounces (males), and measuring from 3¼–4¾ inches from nose to tail tip. They live about a year and a half to two years in captivity, but some have lived four years. Males are the larger sex. Because they are smaller than the Syrians, they are harder to hold. The speed of the wild Campbell's hasn't diminished with captivity. These hamsters move fast.

These are social hamsters, living quite happily together if introduced/put together while they are young. Campbell's bear their young (eight is the average litter size) after a gestation of eighteen to nineteen days, and like other hamsters they tend to be reproducing machines. (In captivity, researcher Francis Ebling found that if Campbell's are placed on a long day cycle of 16 hours of light and 8 hours of dark, the females can give birth again in just 20 days.) Under normal captive conditions the usual time may be as little as 36 days. This means the female can mate successfully when her young are one day old.

Unlike other rodent species, the male Campbell's plays a substantial role in the survival of the young. We are only beginning to realize how important these family bonds can be. Jennifer Jones and Katherine Wynne-Edwards published their observations of the male Campbell's support in the birth and rearing of the young. He assists mechanically during delivery, licks and sniffs the young in the moments after the birth, and opens the pups' airways by clearing the nostrils. The father continues to contribute to pup survival through direct care of the young. He even hops into the nest when the mother is absent (as does an aunt to the young, if a female sibling of the mother is caged with the pair).

As a result of the presence of these adults, pups are very rarely left alone in the nest and so are not subjected to cooling, an important survival factor when the pups are too small to maintain their own body temperature. The young mature rapidly and reach sexual maturity at four weeks.

About the Winter White Hamster

The third type of hamster is the dwarf winter white, *Phodophus sungorus*. Winter whites are from the grassy steppes of eastern Kazakhstan and southwestern Siberia. The areas of origin give a bit of a clue as to the other common names used for this species, which are dwarf hamster, the

winter white Russian dwarf hamster, the Siberian hamster, or the Djungarian hamster, which is why common names aren't always reliable. If you want a specific kind of hamster, look for it under its scientific name to avoid being disappointed.

Winter whites bear the dubious distinction of causing more allergic responses in humans than any other pet hamster species.

Like ermine and snowshoe hares, winter whites in the wild change coat color with the seasons, being dark-furred during the summer and white-furred during the winter. Purebred winter whites will do the same in captivity, providing their caging is illuminated only with natural light. (If you're wanting a winter white, be sure you get a purebred. Some interbreed with Campbell's, and those young won't change color.) This limits you to looking at your winter white's cage during

The discoverer of the winter white, Peter Pallas, wrote of his adventures in Journey through the Various Provinces of Russia in the Years 1768–1773.

daylight hours, however, while the resident is fast asleep inside. He'll become active after the sun goes down and his world becomes properly dark. My winter whites from a long-term breeder in California never became entirely white-furred, but they lost their black side stripe, and their gray coats got whiter and paler as the winter solstice approached.

The hamster was first described (as a type of mouse!) by German naturalist Peter Pallas, who spent six years exploring Siberia, the Urals, and China from 1768–1774. By all rights, the winter white probably should be named for Pallas, but this exclusion won't harm Pallas's good name; several species of birds and mammals were named for him as the result of his explorations.

Like the other hamster types, winter whites were a latecomer to the pet marketplace, first being used as a research animal in a Czechoslovakia laboratory in the 1960s. Two pair were brought to a lab in Germany, and their descendants made their way to the pet market.

In the wild, the winter whites live together in the very broadest sense. Each female shares separate burrows with at least two male winter whites. Those males share burrows with at least two females. When the young are born, the male shares in caring for his young.

During the summer, they are dark gray-brown with a white-to-gray belly. There's a black stripe down the back, and a black stripe on each side separates the gray from the white. As the days grow shorter and winter approaches, their gray coat is shed and replaced by a white coat, but the black dorsal stripe remains. Captive breeding has brought us two other color morphs. One is the sapphire, a blue-gray color with a dark dorsal stripe, white-to-cream belly, and dark eyes. The other is the pearl white, which has a white body, ticked with gray hairs, and a darker head. Neither of these color morphs change their coat color with the short day cycle during the winter.

Physical characteristics: These are small hamsters, with a body length of about 2¼–4 inches (53–102 mm). The tail is about ⅓-inch long (7–11 mm) and is usually tucked into the fur, so you don't see it. They have larger eyes than the Campbell's hamster,

Winter white pairs form monogamous bonds, and the male shows signs of depression if separated from the female.

smaller ears, and slightly thicker fur. Like the Campbell's, they live a year and a half to two years in captivity. The dwarf hamsters are thought to live longer in the wild than in captivity—this unexpected switch may be due to a less varied diet, much less exercise, and stressors that would not be encountered in Siberia.

Despite the fact that these hamsters come from very cold areas, they do not hibernate. Instead, they slip into a morning torpor for a few extra hours of sleep. Their metabolic rate does drop during this sleep, but not enough for it to be considered hibernation. The winter whites must survive on hoarded food and whatever they can gather from the frozen landscape. It seems this sort of edge-existence would stress the animals, but the opposite is true. Researcher Staci Bilbo of Johns Hopkins Hospital in Baltimore and her colleagues have found that those hamsters under short-day regimens (winter days) had more major immune cells and recovered faster from fever than those on long-day cycles (summer days).

These are the social hamsters, living well in small groups or in family groupings. An all-male group will get along best if put together while they are young.

When a pair mates, the four to six young are born after a gestation of eighteen to nineteen days—generally. Both the Campbell's and the winter white hamsters can put pregnancy on "pause" after the mothers have been

fertilized by the males. The process is called postimplantation diaphase, and it means the female parent can delay the onset of pregnancy. One benefit of this delay is that the pups that are currently being fed by the mother will weigh more when they are weaned. In effect, the mother can channel her energy toward the current set of pups instead of dividing that energy between the pups and the embryos growing in her womb. The only other mammals that can do this are bats. The female can also "choose" not to become pregnant; if the male(s) associated with her is removed or killed after mating with her, she will not become pregnant, another indication of the value of the male in family rearing.

Female winter whites can give birth to another litter just twenty four days after the birth of the first. Young

Same-sex winter whites can live together, but if squabbles continue you may need to separate them.

become sexually mature when only a month or so old.

Wynne-Edwards observed litters of both Campbell's and winter white hamsters, and found that unlike the Campbell's hamsters, the winter white fathers rarely spent time in the nest alone with the young, although the male winter white does contribute to the care of the young. The young winter whites grow faster than the Campbell's during the first week or so of birth, probably because the female parent raises the temperature of the nest 2°F (about 4°C) higher than nonbreeding levels. (The mother's resting body temperature is higher when she is with her pups; this adaptation and the ability to not become pregnant are just two of the reasons researchers are finding the winter white hamsters worthy research subjects.) Young *sun-gorus*, more than any other kind of pet trade hamster, need access to drinking water or a water source, like fresh apple, beginning at eight days of age in order to avoid growth retardation.

Winter white pairs form monogamous bonds. Lesley Castro-William and Kathleen Matt found when animals were paired for three weeks then separated, the males demonstrated body and behavior changes that are similar to human depression. The males ate more and gained weight, and were less active, spending more time in their sleeping area and less time exploring their cage.

About the Roborovski Hamsters

The third dwarf hamster, the Roborovski hamster, *Phodophus roborovski*, is less well known than the

Roborovski hamsters are communal if placed together when young.

Syrian and the other dwarf species, but its social nature and petite size have made it a popular choice for those who like responsive, small hamsters.

This is another hamster species that hails from the seemingly inhospitable dry areas of western and eastern Mongolia, China, and the Soviet Union. The Roborovski hamster was discovered in 1894 by Lieutenant Roborovsky but not described until 1903. They weren't kept as a pet until after 1970. They were brought to the United Kingdom from the Netherlands in 1990.

Robos, as they are called, live in groups in single-entrance burrows in flat, sandy areas. They awaken later than the other dwarf hamsters, being most active from 9–10 P.M. They are well adapted to living in cold temperatures and like the Campbell's, can concentrate their urine.

Physical characteristics: Roborovski's are small hamsters, with a body length of about 2 inches. They have a slighter build than either the dwarf Campbell's or the dwarf winter white. The wild color is agouti, a golden brown fur with a gray base on the upper two-thirds of the body, with a dark dorsal stripe (this stripe seems to have disappeared in captive-bred examples). The tail, stomach, legs, nose, and eyebrows are all white, and the pallid eyebrows seem to give this hamster a perpetually quizzical expression. Because these creatures are comparative newcomers to the pet market, there are fewer color morphs. Robo-breeder and Roborovski website creator Dymph Labbé

says there are four color phases of the Robo—the normal agouti, a white-faced agouti whose pelage seems to lighten with age, a pure white Roborovski (this one seems to have more health problems, like the white Syrian), and a mottled phase.

Life span in captivity is three to three and a half years, but some have lived as long as four years. They live well in same-sex pairs.

These are fast-moving hamsters, quick to scurry out of the way when they feel you might actually open their cage. They are so slight in body it can be scary to grasp them for fear something might break. They seem to be a bit more nervous about being petted, although they do tame down well. One

The "rust" Roborovski has a distinct reddish cast to its fur.

The normal coloration for the Roborovski includes white eyebrows and a gray undercoat.

Opposite page: Syrians can live together when young, but adults—like this black-eyed cream—are solitary animals.

Hamster Species (are all members of the subfamily Cricetidae)		
Genus	Common Name	Genus, Species
Cricetus	European field hamster	*Cricetus cricetus*
Cricetulus	Armenian (gray) hamster	*Cricetulus migratorius*
	Ladak	*Cricetulus alticola*
	Chinese striped	*Cricetulus barabensis*
	Mongolian	*Cricetulus curtatus*
	Lesser longtailed	*Cricetulus longicaudatus*
	Greater longtailed	*Cricetulus triton*
	Tibetan	*Cricetulus kamensis*
	Kazah	*Cricetulus eversmani*
	Chinese	*Cricetulus griseus*
	Dark	*Cricetulus obscurus*
	False gray	*Cricetulus pseudogriseus*
Mesocricetus	Syrian	*Mesocricetus auratus*
	Rumanian	*Mesocricetus neutoni*
	Turkish	*Mesocricetus brandti*
	Ciscauscasion	*Mesocricetus raddei*
Mystromys	South African	*Mystromys albicaudatus*
Phodophus	Campbell's	*Phodophus campbelli*
	Winter whites	*Phodophus sungorus*

hamster breeder found her Roborovski hamster would crawl into her hand when she opened the cage door then lie in her hand while she petted it until it fell asleep.

My pair was understandably nippy and agitated about being bothered while they had young. Like other hamster breeds, if the parents think they're being bothered too much, they kill and eat their young. Usual litter size is three to five young, and gestation is twenty to twenty-two days. Breeding and birthing usually occur during the long days, but in captivity the longer days created by artificial lighting means your Robos have the potential to breed more frequently, which is why separation of the sexes make sense.

Once they accept the fact that they aren't in any danger, Robos settle down and will raise their young (if the mother and litter are left alone for the first week or so). They live quite well in family groups, but again, it is best to keep these family groups of a single

sex before they discover each other and babies result. If they seem too wriggly and small to hold while sexing them, put them one at a time in a quart glass jar, and peer at them from underneath (see page 43 on how to sex Robos, and please hurry).

Same-sex groups seem to live together quite nicely, particularly if introduced to each other while they are young. Temporary cage partitions that allow odor transfer and visual contact are a feasible way to introduce newcomers to each other.

About the Chinese Hamster

The fifth hamster in the pet market is the Chinese hamster, *Cricetulus griseus.* This is the very hamster that Saul Adler had been using in his research in the late 1920s.

This hamster comes from northern China and Mongolia. It inhabits rocky terrain and is a good climber. Their burrows are often shallow, perhaps because it's hard to dig a deep burrow in rocky areas, but can be up to 3 feet deep, with sleeping and food chambers branching off from the main tunnel. Their burrows may have two entrances. During spring and summer, all members of this genus are active day and night, but they become more nocturnal as the days shorten. Although they do not hibernate, they do sleep longer during the short day cycle. If discovered, they either freeze in place or run.

These hamsters were kept as pets in China long before they became laboratory animals. In 1919 they were used at Peking Union Medical College for research on the *Pneumococcus* bacteria. Shipments of potential breeding colonies were made to other countries in the Near East, India, and England, and all efforts to breed them failed. Researchers had no idea of how to deal with the aggression of the females toward all other Chinese hamsters or the importance of providing short day and long day cycles. In 1957, a breeding colony was finally established at Harvard University.

Once the techniques of captive breeding had been mastered, Chinese hamsters made the short hop to the pet market. They aren't as popular as the dwarf hamsters or the Syrian, however.

Physical characteristics: The Chinese hamster is one of the nonsocial hamsters, tolerating the presence of another Chinese only of the opposite sex and only long enough to breed.

They are small, slight hamsters, dark gray in color with a darker dorsal stripe. The belly is ivory to gray. Females have four pairs of mammaries. Body length is about 4–5 inches, and their weight is about an ounce, or 43 gms. (Compare this to the Syrians, and you'll see these are slight hamsters indeed.) They carry their long, slender bodies on very short, slender legs. The tail is about twice the length of the Campbell's or the Syrian hamsters, which means it's all of an inch long. There are reports that it uses its tail to help balance itself when scurrying around on rocks. Its cheek pouches are very large.

The male Chinese hamsters have prominent scrotal sacs under their tails, literally as big as their head. (This may be an adaptation to living in a warmer climate and maintaining a viable sperm production by having a cooler production center for the sperm.) Four to five young are in each litter, born after a gestation of twenty to twenty-one days. The young are weaned at twenty-one to twenty-five days, and become sexually mature at eight to twelve weeks.

These are shy hamsters that don't move as quickly as the other species. If your Chinese hamster gets loose, and you can see it, it's easy to shoo into an empty cardboard box, laid on its side, and then gently scoop him up in your hand from the carton.

The term "podophus" refers to the foot pad of the animal, which has a single pad.

Chapter Three
Selecting Your Hamster

What Hamsters Are Like as Pets

Hamsters have an acute sense of smell. They love to explore their surroundings, they are curious about everything, and if you give them a minute to wake up, they don't even mind awakening out of a deep snooze to visit with you.

They interact with each other and can identify each other by scent. They will shred up paper towels, explore their cage, check out what's new in the food dish, and run in their wheel for hours at a time. They are always interested in their surroundings, and if they could just juggle that cage door open a bit, they'd check out *your* surroundings as well.

Hamsters will sit in your hands for a few minutes, and if you let your hamster get to know you, he'll even fall asleep in your hands. But then they'd like to get back in their cage, to familiar surroundings.

If cost is a factor, hamster keeping does not require a lot of money.

A wire and plastic hamster cage is probably the easiest and the best choice for caging most hamsters. Because of their small size, the Roborovski hamsters need to be kept in a solid cage, like an aquarium tank, with a screened lid. "Bin" cages are becoming more popular, but you have to make the modifications yourself, so they generally aren't something you can buy and use right away. Buy the biggest cage you have space for.

The animal itself is not expensive, if you buy it. Sometimes you can "rehome" a hamster that someone else no longer wants, and the cost is very small. Even if the animal is free, remember that hamsters are worthy, responsive pets and must never be thought to be "expendable." If you are looking for a specific breed, coat, and color, you may need to order from a breeder, and the shipping costs will be in addition to the cost of the animal.

All-in-one chow-style food is not expensive, and a three-month supply will take up about as much space as a large cereal box.

Any costs associated with a veterinary visit are hard to estimate. You'll have the charge for the office visit(s), but any medication, diagnostic tests, or other lab work will be an additional cost. Do consider putting some funds aside to help offset these costs. Your hamster can seem to be extremely well one moment and the next he's lying on his side, outside of his sleeping area,

they found him strolling along the top of the sofa, evidently the place he'd been for a year. He'd been able to steal enough food and find water (probably from the refrigerator evaporation pan) during all that time. Hamsters can be smarter than we might think. Don't give yours a chance to upstage you.

All in all, the cost of hamster ownership is less than the cost of a dog or a cat, and you don't have to take him out for a walk, or pick up after him or her. You will have gained a charming companion who enjoys exploring your pockets and taking sunflower seeds from your fingers. He won't borrow money from you and forget to repay it. He won't chew up your shoes. What a bargain you've made!

What to Look For in a Pet Hamster

What Kind to Buy

Do you want a calm hamster, one that will seem to enjoy being held and that will willingly crawl out of its opened cage door and into your hands, even if it's only for a minute or two? Then you'll want a Syrian hamster, long considered the best hamster for children.

If you want a beautifully marked hamster, one that's tame, small and rounded in shape, but still quick on its feet, you'll want a Campbell's hamster.

If you like the shape of a Campbell's, but you like a bit of a change

and panting. When you need a veterinarian, you need a veterinarian.

Additional toys, accessories, chew treats, and exercise balls will add to your basic set-up costs.

What's the time cost? Your hamster doesn't need much time, just a half hour a day spent with you, exploring your neckline, your sleeves, your desktop or sofa. Watch your little Houdini—he can squeeze into the tiniest places and "escape" right before your eyes. One hamster did just that—the family moved during the ensuing year, thinking they'd lost him, and gave up on finding their hamster entirely. One day

now and then, you may want a winter white, the dwarf hamster that pales from brownish gray to brownish white during the winter and back to its summertime color in the spring.

If you want a very small hamster that wears its white eyebrow patches as if in perpetual surprise, you'll want a Roborovski hamster. This is a very pretty hamster that lives well in single-sex groups, but it is not the hamster for a child—it is just too fast. Their agility in wiggling out of hands can feel like trying to hold live Jell-O.

If you want to keep more than one hamster and don't want to set up separate cages for each individual, you may want to try small single-breed and probably single-sex groups of Campbell's or the winter whites.

These live well in small groups, particularly if they've been brought up together, although you may hear some squeaked discussions at night.

If you like the idea of a long-haired hamster, then one of the long-haired Syrians may be the pet for you. You may end up actually trimming the coat if it catches up too much litter or shavings; brushing or combing tends to pull out the hair rather than remove the tangles. You'll really notice this if the hamster is a male; the males' coats are longer than the females'.

So you've done a bit of research, and you are fairly certain you want a Syrian, one as close to the standard golden color as you can find. But, the pet store also has some pretty Campbell's.

A dove mottled Campbell's hamster has red eyes.

the hamster, using your fingers to form a cage around the hamster. Compress your hands slightly so both palms can feel the hamster, and move your fingers so he can't squeeze through them. Be aware that a hamster when first held may produce a loud squeak and then try to launch itself between your fingers and out of your hands like a wet water balloon. Hamsters are very skilled at this, so expect it.

The second method is one I've used rarely because my hamsters just hated it. It is the nape hold. You put your hand over the hamster, pinning it place against the substrate, and use your thumb and forefinger to grasp the nape of its neck. Lift the hamster, and let its body slide down inside its skin, a little like a golfball inside a sock. This hold takes practice, although it does immobilize the hamster so you can sex it.

The third hold is another one-hand hold, one that makes it hard for the hamster to twist around and bite your fingers. You place your hand over the hamster, with its head between your middle and forefinger. Your thumb and forefinger are on one side of its body, and your middle, ring finger, and pinkie are on the other. Curl your fingers slightly and pick him up, turning your hand so your hamster faces you. This puts the hamster on his back, in the palm of your hand. Some hamster keepers feel this hold is too restrictive and uncomfortable for the hamster.

Once you have the hamster in hand, see how the hamster responds to you. Does it seem to enjoy being held, per-

How do you decide? You simply pick the one you like the best—and you decide in part, by carefully holding the prospects, even for just a minute or two. Ask the pet store employee or the breeder to take it out of the cage for you, or if you feel you can maneuver the hamster out of his cage (some of those door openings are small!), pick it up yourself. If you're taking the hamster out of its cage, try to scoop it up in your hand from behind, or put a small dish in the cage and shoo it into the dish, then empty the dish into your hand.

There are three ways to pick up and hold a hamster. The one most useful and easiest to do uses both hands. You shoo the hamster onto one hand with the other and then cup your hand over

haps after a few moments of trying to get through your fingers? Does it nestle into your hand and then look upward toward your face?

Don't reject a hamster because it flops over onto its back and bares its teeth as your hand approaches it. He's scared. Give that hamster a few minutes to calm down, and try again, making certain that this time you've washed your hands so you don't bring in any possible odors from another hamster.

If you can, hold at least three, so you can select the one you like the best. It's best to avoid buying one that nips you. Of course, you can probably tame it, but you can also buy a hamster that doesn't nip, from the start.

If the pet store doesn't want you to hold their hamsters prior to picking one to purchase, thank them, and try another pet store. You and your hamster will be together for the rest of its life, and you need one that you'll enjoy owning and handling.

Picking a Healthy Hamster

The basic rules for picking a healthy hamster are the same as any other mammal. No matter what species you select, look for one with bright eyes and an inquisitive attitude. Unless you're buying an alien hamster—the hairless morph of the Syrians—look for a hamster with a full, even coat. Be sure to check its anus for any signs of wetness; this could be a sign of wet-tail. This is not considered bad manners, a hamster with wet-tail is not a healthy hamster.

As you hold the hamster, take a moment to run your fingers lightly over its shoulders and hips. Any lumps or tender spots? Tell the sales associate if you suspect any, and select another hamster.

Does age matter? Any species of hamster you buy has an expected life span of eighteen months to two years (Roborovskis may live three years). If you want to spend every possible moment with your hamster, from weaning through old age (the hamster's, that is), buy a young one. There are very few things cuter than a baby hamster of any kind. Certainly it's easy to get a very young hamster to adapt to you and your household.

If you feel that a year is long enough to spend with a hamster, go for the adult. If for any reason the adult you get doesn't seem tame, just work with him or her for a few minutes at least once a day; hamsters can remember

Winter white hamsters were thought to be a type of mouse when first described.

odors from other hamsters for only twenty four hours, so don't give yours the chance to "forget" you. However, if you think that having a hamster for only a year or so will ease the heartache when it goes to the great hamster wheel in the sky, think again. It would be hard not to fall in love with a small, alert, bright-eyed creature that regards you as a bringer of good things, a creature that never has to be taken outside, never has to get expensive inoculations, won't make so much noise your neighbors complain, and won't destroy your house while you're away. Having a hamster-sized hole in your heart can be very uncomfortable.

Which sex is better? It doesn't really matter. Males are never pregnant when you buy them, so if you do buy a male you won't be surprised by babies a few weeks later. Male and female hamsters both make good companions. There are physical differences between the males and females of course; one of my friends declined the offer of a male Chinese hamster because she didn't like the way he looked (the male Chinese hamsters are the ones with the very noticeable testicles). If you want more than one hamster and you want to keep them together, you'll probably want a same-sex grouping of one of the communal species. Perhaps a female grouping would be more harmonious than a male grouping, although it can be possible to keep both types with no problems.

Roborovski hamsters will live in same-sex groupings.

Sources of Hamsters

Where you get your hamster depends to a great degree on how long you've thought about the process. The costs begin at zero and go up from there.

Once in a while your local animal shelter will have a hamster up for adoption. The usual adoption fee may be small, about $5, or may be waived for small rodents.

Some people acquire their hamster rather as a spur-of-the-moment impulse. The classified ads in your local newspaper do occasionally have "hamsters free to a good home" ads, and company bulletin boards are another source of these ads. Children tend to

The two-hand hamster hold takes a bit of practice in order to make both parties feel secure.

be vulnerable to acquiring pets. Your child may be capable of assuring you he doesn't know *where* he got the hamster-with-cage now sitting in his room.

The impulse hamsters tend to be low-cost or free. Usually the cage and the food/bedding are added as an inducement. Of course, you can't choose the one you like—you take what's available.

The next step up in hamster acquisition is the pet store. Hamsters from a pet store are modestly priced, and the cost of cage/bedding/feeding dishes/feed tend to be added on to that original animal price. As a special promotion, some pet stores will throw in (not literally, I'm sure) a hamster when you buy the hamster setup. This can seem to make the hamster less valuable, however: "After all, the hamster didn't

cost me anything." But the dispassionate bargain attitude toward the hamster is only temporary, until you see how children respond to the personality and shoe-button eyes, and discover what fun this furry little dynamo can be during its waking hours.

You can be fairly certain that the hamster you buy from a pet store will be in good health and good condition. They are usually maintained in one-hamster cages, with little to no chance of biting each other, spreading diseases, or becoming pregnant. Ask if there is any sort of a health guarantee for your purchase; one of my local big-box pet stores had a fourteen-day health guarantee, which came in useful when the Syrian I bought came down with wet-tail two days later. Another big-box chain actually had me sign an "as-is" agreement when I bought

The nape hold was universally disliked by all of my hamsters, but it is a quick way to move them from cage to cage.

a pocket pet from them—and it was sick two days later (no, I never bought another animal from them).

But if your pet store sells hamsters from a communal cage, this doesn't necessarily mean the pet store is careless. Hamsters can get along temporarily under what we'd consider very crowded (more than three per cage) conditions. The adults get along in sort of a forced peace, agreeing not to fight for now but willing to change that rule if anyone starts acting up. That being said, young born under crowded cage conditions rarely survive the night.

Once hamsters get away from the crowded caging, things may change.

Females purchased from a communal cage and given proper housing, good food, and a bit of bedding in a snug corner of their own cage, can surprise you with a litter anywhere from a week to two weeks post-purchase (the term is "postimplatation diaphase," page 27). (Remember, if you hear squeaking, don't bother the mom or her babies. This means stay *away* from the cage except to provide food and water for at least a week.)

The advantage of buying from a pet store is that you're assured that your hamster has been given good food and housing while it has been in the store and that you'll have some good advice on the sex of your hamster. If you buy from a pet store, you'll have the help of the staff on what caging and supplies to buy, and you can take everything home with you. The staff wants you to be happy with your new pet, and hopes you will return to the store soon for food and play gear, and perhaps another, larger cage.

If you're incredibly lucky, you'll be able to attend a hamster show or find a professional breeder near you (or if you don't mind waiting a day or so and live near an airport, you can have your hamster shipped to you, but few beginner hamster keepers want to go to that much trouble or expense). A breeder is a treasure several times over. She or he knows hamsters like no one you may have ever met. Professional breeders keep records, generation after generation of records. They know what lines ought not to breed with what lines (see pages 49, 92, and 93 as to why this is important); they know what colors are popular and what shades are new; they know the latest on commercial hamster foods and will gladly tell you what they use and why; they have hamsters of different ages, so you can buy an adult if you want an adult; or you can buy a young hamster. They know where and when the next show will be held, so you might ask about the next show, if only to see if hamster breeders are as *feverish* about their hobby as are the orchid breeders. (But be warned— being tempted is part of going to a show—see Chapter 9 for more about shows.) The best thing about the professional breeders is that they really like hamsters, they really care for and about their hamsters, and they've bred their lines for specific qualities.

You may be gingerly feeling in the direction of your wallet, and asking, "But aren't those professionals a lot more expensive than pet stores?" They aren't appreciably more expensive, at least not for a pet hamster. Much like show dogs, oh, how can this be said without sounding coldhearted, not every hamster in a litter is a show-quality hamster, and those less-than-show-quality hamsters are what the breeder is happy to sell to individuals and to pet stores. Instead of buying a hamster that looks like every other hamster you've seen from a pet store, you'll have a hamster from a known lineage, from a hamster breeder who prides herself/himself in breeding for

temperament *and* show-quality coat/ color/conformation. A terrific bargain for you—and for the lucky hamster you take home. Who would settle for a plain brown Campbell's when you could have an umbrous black tortoise-shell?

You may be able to get a retired hamster, a former breeder. Some hamster breeds live far longer than their breeding effectiveness (Syrians have a useful breeding life of one year and generally can live a year or so beyond that).

Hamsters, like this golden umbrous Syrian, seem to enjoy time spent with their owners.

Sexing Hamsters

Some hamster species are very easy to sex—you can just look at Chinese hamsters and sex them; the males have very large testicles. The other hamster types need to be held to be sexed.

For the Syrians, the Campbell's, and the Roborovski hamsters, grasp them gently but firmly around the body and lift them up. Hamsters don't like being held almost upright, leaning back a tad, so the hamster may struggle. Hold fast to the hamster. If he wriggles too much inside his skin for you to be comfortable, you can try the famous nape hold, but watch out—you could get bitten. It may be easier to just put your fingers under the hamster's armpits, lift him up, and then support his fat little body with your other hand.

When you have your hamster immobilized, look at the genital area, the lower belly where the tail meets the body. Female hamsters have the genital opening and the anus close together, perhaps a quarter inch or so apart, one right above the other.

Males have the genital opening separated from the anal opening by a distance about equal to the width of your forefinger. And in males older than five weeks, when you hold him upright, the testes fall down to the edge of the body to form two distinct pale pink lumps on each side of the anus.

What Color Is My Hamster?

Thanks to the patience and skill of breeders, hamsters come in far more colors than the basic brown-gold of the Syrians and the brown-gray of the Campbell's. They now are available in several coat textures and patterns that are independent of the colors.

You can basically pick a color, a pattern, and a coat texture, and find a Syrian or a Campbell's to match. The winter whites, Chinese, and Roborovski hamsters have far fewer colors and coats to select from.

Exercising even more skill, the breeders have a name and a description for every color, pattern, and coat morph. To see what sort of hamster you probably have, pick up your hamster and thumb through the following list. Don't be upset if you can't actually match up the hamster in your hand with the descriptions. Breeders (particularly backyard breeders, those who breed hamsters only to get more hamsters) tend to form their own definition of some of the colors, and unless you know what the parents looked like, you won't know

the genetic background of your hamster. New colors seem to appear on a fairly regular basis.

Start by deciding the color of your hamster's coat. Just because your hamster is an overall pale gray doesn't mean your hamster is pale gray all the way through. Use your fingers to part your hamster's fur, and notice the color of the fur at the tips and next to the body.

Syrian Colors

Golden: Like the wild form, the fur of the modern golden Syrian is banded, dark gray at the roots and a golden brown at the tips. You can't call it an agouti color, because agouti coloration means a black tip to the hair shaft. There is a dark line that extends from the bottom

Banded Syrians are still the most popular coat pattern.

"Black bear" Syrians always have white feet.

A chocolate Syrian hamster has dark ears and white feet.

of the face, just under the ears, and back over the shoulders, and the cheeks are usually white. The ears are dark gray, the belly is ivory, and the eyes dark.

Black: The animal is entirely black, with the exception of white feet, gray ears, and dark eyes. The fur is black from root to tip. This is the hamster called the "black bear" by some hamster breeders and pet stores. A black banded hamster (black with white belly band) may be sold as a panda hamster.

Blue: This is dark gray color that cropped up unexpectedly in a group of Syrians in a pet store in Lisbon, Portugal (hamster people are quite chatty on HamsterCentral.com, and unexpected finds are always of interest), in 2009 or so. It's a solid or self color.

Brown (dove): The fur is pale brown from the roots to the tips. The belly is ivory. The ears are pale, and the eyes are red. The eyes darken with age, but in a flashlight beam are still a burgundy color.

Chocolate (a color to love): There are two shades of chocolate. The sable form has fur that's pale milk chocolate with *paler* roots. The ears are gray and the eyes dark. The black chocolate is a dark chocolate fur from root to tip. The feet are white. The ears are gray and the eyes dark.

Cinnamon: The attractive ginger color conceals a blue-gray undercoat; the belly is ivory. The ears are pale, and the eyes are red.

Copper: The body fur is a deep copper with darker roots. Fur around the eyes is paler copper, and the ears are pale. The eyes are red. The eyes darken with age but in a flashlight beam are still a burgundy color.

Cream with black eyes: The fur is cream to the roots. The cream becomes a bit more tan in tone as the animal matures. The ears are gray and the eyes dark.

Cream with red eyes: The fur is pink-toned cream from root to tip, and the color intensifies as the animal matures. The ears are pale, and the eyes are red, darkening with age.

Gray (dark): The fur is gray with darker roots. The belly is ivory. The "cheek streak" is black.

Gray (light): Pale gray fur with dark gray roots. The muzzle is almost white, and the cheek streak is dark brown-gray. The belly is ivory. The ears are dark, and the eyes are black.

Gray (silver): The fur is silvery-gray with dark gray roots. The belly is ivory. The ears are dark, and the eyes are black.

Honey: Color is a cream variant, varying from yellow-orange to an orange-cream with cream roots. The eyes are red and ears are pale. The belly is cream, and a darker cheek flash separates the belly color from the deeper color on the back. Coloration of the back and the eyes darkens with age.

Ivory with black eyes: The fur is almost but not quite white from root to tip; the ears are gray, the eyes dark.

Ivory with red eyes: The fur is almost but not quite white from root to tip; the ears are pale, the eyes are red and may darken to burgundy with age.

Lilac: the fur is gray with a lavender tone, which may take on a brown coloration as the animal matures. The roots are gray. The belly is ivory. The ears are pale, and the eyes are red.

Pearl (smoke): Fur is pale gray at the root, darkening to black at the tip. The belly is ivory. Ears are gray, and the eyes are black.

Rust: Almost a copper color but a bit browner, with gray roots. The ears are gray, and the eyes are dark. This color is rarely available in the United States, although some breeders have selectively bred their Syrians for a rustlike color, the color does not breed true.

Sable: The fur is black with cream roots. There are cream circles around the eyes. As the animal matures, the black may fade to brown or dark gray. The eyes are dark.

Sable Roan: Fur is white with sable hairs ticked throughout. The head is

The honey Syrian is yellow-orange with a darker flash under the eye and red eyes.

The sable banded Syrian has bands of dark coffee color, but the undercoat is pale.

darker, but the ears are pale. The eyes are black.

Tortoiseshell: This hamster is the result of a cross between a yellow and another color.

When yellow is bred with black, and the offspring bred with white, you get a hamster that looks like a calico cat, with patches of reddish brown, white, and black. Interestingly enough, most tortoiseshell hamsters are females, the males are very rare, just like the cats.

Umbrous Golden: Like the golden hamster, but the golden areas are tinged with a gray overcoat and the belly is gray.

White with dark ears: The fur is white from root to tip. The ears are dark and turn even darker as the animal ages. The eyes are red.

White with pale ears: This is the result of a cross between the Dark-eared White and the Cinnamon. The fur is pure white. The ears are pale and the eyes red.

Yellow: The fur is yellow-tan with dark tips. The black tipping seems to intensify with age. The ears are dark, and the eyes are black.

Yellow Black: This is a cross between the yellow and black. The fur is yellow and heavily tipped with black. The feet are paler than the body. The ears are gray, and the eyes are dark.

Tiffany is a tortoiseshell Syrian.

Coat Patterns

Self: Any solid color. Sometimes the feet may be paler.

Banded: This is a combination between a white and any other color. The white is on the belly and in a band across the back. The band may or may not be solid—it may be interrupted by the other color.

Dominant Spot: This is white combined with a color to produce a hamster with a white belly and a white-with-color-splotched back. The splotches are most obvious on the side of the body.

Roan: The fur is any color, mixed with white hairs. The base color is most distinct on the head.

Tortoiseshell: Yellow coat, heavily dotted with black. This is a sex-linked gene, meaning it is found on female hamsters only.

Recessive Dapple: White hamster with colored head, white blaze, and colored rump.

Coat

There are five Syrian coat types, although it can be hard to tell if you're dealing with a coat type or a color.

Hairless: Also called the alien hamster. There is no fur on the body with the possible exception of whiskers. Alien females often do not produce enough milk to feed their young.

Short or normal coat: A short coat with no texture.

Long-haired: The fur is long, sometimes as long as 4 inches in areas. The males have the longer coats; often the females have only a long "skirt."

Yellow-black Syrians have a yellow undercoat with black tipping.

Rex: The fur curls upward, both in short-haired and long-haired forms. Even the whiskers are curly. With the short-haired forms, the result is a plush-looking hamster. With the long-haired forms, it's a bit like Einstein meets

The Syrian long-haired banded panda.

49

static electricity. Don't breed a Rex to a Rex—the eyelashes are curly and often turned in, against the eye, which may result in painful corneal ulcers. (Eyelashes are hair, and hair can scratch or abrade the eyeball, causing a lesion or ulcer in the cornea.)

Satin: The hair, although sparse, has a very glossy appearance.

Umbrose: The umbrose gene adds a layer of gray atop any color, creating a slightly darker hamster.

Campbell's Coat Colors

Normal: The fur is brown-gray, with dark roots. A dark stripe runs from the head to the tail. The belly is white. The ears are gray, and the eyes are dark.

Normal, with mottling: The fur is white with patches of brown-gray. The dorsal stripe is dark but may not be complete. The belly is white. The ears are gray, and the eyes are dark or red.

The red eyes in color variants like this Campbell's may darken with age.

Normal, with platinum: Fur is brown-gray with white hairs sprinkled throughout. The ears are pale, and the eyes are black.

Albino: The fur is white from root to tip. There is no dorsal stripe. Ears are pale, and the eyes are red.

Argente, with red eyes: The fur is reddish-brown or cinnamon with blue-gray roots. The dorsal stripe is a muted dark gray. The belly is white. Ears are pale, and the eyes are red.

Argente, with black eyes: The fur is pale reddish-brown or cinnamon with gray roots. The dorsal stripe is dark gray. The belly is white. Ears are gray, and the eyes are black.

Argente, mottled: The fur is mottled white with cinnamon; the cinnamon portions have blue-gray roots. The dorsal stripe is a muted dark gray and may not be complete. The belly is white. Ears are pale, and the eyes are red.

Beige: This is a cross between the argente and the black-eyed argente. The fur is pale orange-beige, and the dorsal stripe is darker. The belly and muzzle are white. The ears are pale, and the eyes are red.

Blue Fawn: The fur is reddish-brown with a blue tint. The roots are blue-gray, as is the dorsal stripe. Belly is ivory. Ears are pale, and the eyes are red.

Black: Fur is very dark gray to black from root to tip. The dorsal stripe is darker than the fur but barely visible. The feet and chin are white. The ears are gray and the eyes black.

Black, mottled: Fur is mottled white with patches of dark gray to black. The dorsal stripe is barely visible. The feet and chin are white. The ears are black and white, and the eyes are black.

Blue: This is a cross between opal and black. The fur is gray-blue, and the dorsal stripe is darker but largely indistinct. The ears are gray, and the eyes are black.

Blue, mottled: The fur is gray-blue with white patches. The dorsal stripe is darker but largely indistinct. The ears are gray, and the eyes are black.

Blue Fawn: This is a cross between opal and argente. The fur is blue-tan in color. The dorsal stripe is darker but indistinct. The ears are pale, and the eyes are red.

Chocolate: This is a cross between the black-eyed argente and the black. The fur is a medium brown, rather a pale milk chocolate color, with a slightly darker dorsal strip. The eyes are black.

Dove: This is a cross between the black and argente. The fur is gray, with a slightly darker dorsal stripe. The belly is ivory. The ears are pale, and the eyes are red. The eyes darken with age but in a flashlight beam are still a burgundy color.

Dove, mottled: The fur is gray with white patches. The dorsal stripe is indistinct. The belly is ivory. The ears are pale, and the eyes are red. The eyes darken with age but flash red in a flashlight beam.

Lilac Fawn: this is a cross between opal and the black-eyed argente. The fur is blue-tan, and the dorsal stripe is a slightly darker shade. The ears are pale, and the eyes are black.

Opal: Fur is blue-gray with ivory belly and muzzle. Sides are tan. Dorsal stripe is slightly darker. Ears are gray, and the eyes are dark.

Opal mottled: Fur is blue-gray with white patches and white belly and muzzle. Dorsal stripe is slightly darker and not distinct. Ears are pale to gray, and the eyes are dark.

Opal Platinum: Fur is blue-gray with white hairs mixed in. Belly and muzzle are white, but these don't contrast as strongly as in the darker Opal. Dorsal stripe is dark but indistinct. Ears are gray, and the eyes are dark.

White with black eyes: Also called a Dilute Platinum. Fur is white, and there is no dorsal stripe. Ears are white, and the eyes are dark.

White with red eyes: Fur is white, and there is no dorsal stripe. Ears are white, and the eyes are red.

Opal Campbell's hamsters have tan sides with ivory bellies and muzzles.

Chapter Four
Your Hamster's Home

Hamster caging can be expensive or inexpensive, lavish or plain. As long as a few basic parameters are met, your hamster will live its allotted two to three years as a contented and busy hamster who's lucky enough to have a doting owner.

Your hamster needs a safe cage that provides room to run around and things to do; he needs food, a place to sleep, a place to defecate, and clean water.

None of these are particularly hard to supply. The only caveat you need to remember is that hamsters are chewers and escape artists. (Israel Aharoni, page 10, learned the hard way. You don't have to.) Hamsters can, if they decide they want to, chew through wood or soft plastic, like the plastic screening on a tank top. Small hamsters, like the Roborovski's, can wriggle through the bars on a bird/hamster cage. For everyone's happiness, provide a cage that at least is difficult to chew out of, and provide toys/chew sticks so your hamster has something to do.

Size and Placement First

Before you select a cage for your hamster, think about size and placement.

Size is important. In Europe, hamster keepers are becoming insistent on a cage with a footprint that's at least 2 square feet. In the United States, a cage that's 12 inches wide by 15 inches long by 12 inches high would be passable for one dwarf hamster, or for a single Syrian. Walk past the colorful little cages that are smaller in size than a 5-gallon terrarium. If manufacturers think there's a market for an inexpensive "cute" small cage, they'll make it.

Just because the cage has been manufactured and it's cute and it's for sale, doesn't make it a good cage for your hamster. Remember that hamsters evolved as ground-dwelling vagabonds. Provide a roomy cage for your hamster, the biggest one you can afford, both money-and space-wise. Recent research by Katerina Fischer, Sabine G. Gebhardt-Henrich, and Andreas Steiger at the Institute of Animal Genetics, Nutrition and Housing in Bern, Switzerland, showed that hamsters in larger cages, just about a yard square (1 meter), showed less cage bar gnawing, less protracted wheel running, and had lower stress levels (measured by elevated body temperature, certainly a valid method—your body temp goes up and you perspire more when you're stressed).

Hamsters with sufficiently large cages tend to spend more time exploring their cages than hamsters in small cages, and consequently spend less time in their wheel. Even after you have your caging set up, if your hamster spends all his time in his wheel, you might rethink the size of the cage you've provided. Although some hamster keepers (and some researchers) don't feel the endless wheel is obsessive, they themselves aren't confined to a small room for their lifetime. The average Syrian hamster will run 5.1 miles (8.3 km; if you figure the human stride at 24 inches, that's about 13,500 steps) a day in his wheel—but this number will go up if the hamster is stressed by loud music, if he is handled roughly, or if he is restricted in a small cage for ten minutes.

Think of cage placement while you're looking at sizes. Place the cage where it is easy to access/clean and easy for you to enjoy your hamster. This may be in your living room, in your bedroom, or in your den/office. If putting your hamster's cage where you can see it and smell it readily means you'll have to be more vigilant in cage cleaning, that's not a bad thing.

Cage Design

There are many ready-made cage designs that are well suited for your hamster. Wire mesh or wire-barred cages are both good choices.

Birdcages make adaptable hamster caging, providing that the bars are close enough together to avoid any escapes. Secure all the sliding doors, even those over the feeding cups. Hamsters are good at figuring things out. You may think you've fastened all those doors shut so only you can open them, but you aren't in a cage 24 hours a day with nothing to do but figure out possible escape routes. (If you haven't heard the stories that begin "We had a hamster, and one day it got out...," you will.) Buy sliding latches, the kind that are on dog leashes, and use them on each door. Hamsters aren't strong enough to push the slide back.

Replace the feeding cups that come with a birdcage with a food dish that sits on the floor of the cage. Those plastic feeding dishes that come with a birdcage are a bit too high off the floor of the cage to allow for easy dining. If the food dish is large enough for your hamster to climb into, that's okay, too. He will probably move most of his food into his bed where he can keep a very close eye on it (there's nothing personal here; it's just what hamsters do).

Birdcages are large enough for you to add an exercise wheel. If the cage has a wire grid above the bottom (and some hamster cages are *sold* with these grids), remove the grid so your hamster can wander about on the solid floor of the cage without hurting his feet. The floor bars are too far apart to permit your hamster to walk about on the cage floor with any sort of comfort (it's like asking you to walk barefoot across a floor littered with pencils), and all his seeds, treats, and stolen

food items will fall through the bars where he can't reach them. Researchers have found that hamsters show a strong preference for solid-floor cages with bedding over barren, wire mesh–floored cages, in case you wondered.

For years people have used repurposed 10-gallon aquarium tanks with clip-on screen tops as cages for hamsters. They were hyped as keeping the hamster safe from drafts, and it would be hard for the hamster to escape. The tanks are easy to set up and easy to clean. Odors are largely contained. Size-wise, these would work for a pair of Roborovski hamsters, but you may find that these are too deep to allow for proper ventilation. Thus, use a repurposed aquarium only temporarily, cleaning it daily so your Robos don't have to smell their own waste.

There is sort of a blend between the birdcage and the aquarium, and that's where the wire part of the cage fits on top of an aquarium. A ramp or access tube runs from a hole in the floor of the top cage through the hardware cloth flooring to a point near the bottom of the aquarium. You add a couple of inches of aspen shavings to the bottom, to allow for burrowing as desired. The exercise wheel, water bottle, and food dish are included in the birdcage portion.

You can buy these units, or you can take apart a wire-type hamster cage and put the wire top on top of an aquarium. I made one of these conversion setups (see page 52) when I wanted to give my Syrian more spaces to explore.

This two-level cage gives a hamster both a semiprivate bottom portion and an "open" area. This sort of multilevel cage does mean you can get more square footage in a small footprint. You do need to be careful to make any sort of a ramp hamster-safe (which is why the tubes are useful here). Hamsters are terrible climbers, in that they like to climb up on bars of the cage or onto a ramp, but they are not at all good about figuring out how to get down. Falls are not good for hamsters.

One cage manufacturer, Qute, has created a two-level cage good-looking enough to put in your living room. The lower shelf section is the sleeping area, filled partially with shavings, connected to the top portion with a plastic tube. The food, exercise wheel, water, and wire door are in the wire-barred top shelf. Either the top or bottom portion can be removed for easy access to your pet or cleaning.

Because I found my homemade two-level cage difficult to clean, I went to a roomy (24 inches long, 13 inches wide, 15 inches high) commercial pet cage with a 5-inch-deep bin and a birdcage-type top. Humboldt was still able to stand atop the shavings in one corner to push out items he no longer wanted. He pushed out empty sunflower kernels, soiled paper towel bits, and, when I replaced the sand in his toilet with red sand, he pushed out the red sand.

If you are the least bit handy, or know someone who is, you can adapt prefab items for caging. IKEA makes an all-glass curio cabinet, about 16 inches square and just over 5 feet high. When the inside glass shelves are removed, the unit turned on one side, and the glass door removed from what is now the top, one has a long hamster

Your hamster may enjoy a sleeping box from a pet store.

cage too high to jump out of (if you keep climbable items away from the sides) with a large footprint. Be sure to add a screen top if you have other pets in your house, and keep the substrate deep. Deep substrate allows for digging and helps with cage ventilation. If you live in a hot climate, do add a small fan blowing across the top of this sort of caging to stir the air inside.

You may want to look at one of the plastic hamster cages, the ones that incorporate the word "trail" in the cage name. Keep in mind these are, by and large, small cages. They come in bright colors and offer a wire or plastic top that clicks onto a plastic base, very visually appealing to humans. Add-on plastic tubes snake out of one side and connect to another side or to the top, to special viewing bins on the side or a top-side access panel. All that I've seen include an exercise wheel, but plan to add one if your caging doesn't come with it. Buy the biggest cage you can, remembering that you're trying to do better than the minimalist 1.4-square-foot footprint. The barred sections do provide ventilation.

These plastic cages seem to have been the impetus for a veritable explosion of accessories beyond the tubes. Manufacturers have spared nothing in bringing out colored water bottles that hang on the outside of the cage, plastic viewing hemisphere bubbles, extra snap-on running wheels, plastic sleeping houses; they've even created rolling hamster balls and hamster motorcycles (this one is powered by an

When You Need Temporary Housing

Plastic shoe boxes or sweater boxes can be used for travel or hamster show cages, if you add circulation. The easiest way to do this is by cutting pieces out of the side and the top and riveting in one-eighth-inch pieces of hardware cloth to cover the holes. (Using a riveter is like using a single hole punch—it isn't hard to use.) You can drill additional holes in the sides. A water bottle will go on the top, with the drinking tube being pushed through the wire mesh so the hamster can reach the tube to drink.

These cages are fine for short-term use, but the limited size and low headroom is going to stress your hamster. Neither the shoe nor the sweater box is high enough for an exercise wheel, and there's no room for toys in the shoe box. Low boxes are only suitable for temporary housing.

exercise wheel). If you keep communal types like Campbell's or winter whites, you can use the tunnels to connect their cages. Some hamster keepers run tunnels around the top of a room.

If you do buy one of the rolling hamster balls, or the rolling hamster-powered motorcycle, don't let your hamster use them unsupervised on a warm day, or on a sunny day in a room with lots of windows. Keep in mind that your hamster's body temperature

goes up when he's stressed, so you want to provide cooler temperatures when he's in the ball. These exercise "wheels" have no water source, and your hamster could become too warm if allowed to stay in the wheel too long. It is very difficult to get comfortable in an exercise wheel, which is why they are named exercise wheels.

Newer in the world of hamster keeping is the bin cage. This is exactly what it says—a repurposed plastic bin with ventilation added in the sides and top. A good basic size is 24 inches long and 12 inches wide at the bottom. Use a utility knife to carefully cut pieces out of the sides and the top. You might offset the removed pieces in the sides

to avoid possible drafts, but really, how cold and windy does your house get? I would suggest keeping the ventilation opening on one end high enough to contain the wood shavings in his sleeping area. If you prefer, you can use a drill to make the ventilation holes in the short sides.

The top may be of stronger plastic than the bin, so be especially careful when you are cutting out the ventilation sections.

You can use one-eighth-inch pieces of hardware cloth to cover the holes on the outside of the bin, securing them with a rivet gun or short nuts and bolts. You'll need to drill holes in the perimeter of the openings to accommodate the rivets or the bolts. I used size 10–24 ½–inch bolts and nuts, putting the round head portion on the *inside* of the cage; a $^3/_8$–inch combo might have worked as well.

Add a slightly larger hole for the tube of the drinking bottle, and two smaller holes for the wire or string to hold the bottle upright, and your new cage is ready.

Hamster Caging— What Goes Inside

Water Bottle

Hamsters must have clean water available to them at all times. In a pinch, you can offer water in a small crock or plastic jar lid, but this isn't going to work long-term. Hamsters fill up water dishes with whatever they can find in their cage, rather on the cheerful attitude of "Well! Let's just bustle right in and fix that big wet spot and keep this cage from getting soggy!"

Go out and buy a laboratory water bottle. They are plastic or sometimes glass bottles, with a hard rubber cork or a screw top and a metal drinking tube. You fill the bottle with water, screw on the top or wedge the cork in the mouth, and hook the bottle on the side of the cage. The drinking tube extends into the cage at a level where the hamster can reach it. Check the water level every other day. If the bottle is suddenly empty, you'll want to check to make sure the bottle did not simply

empty all the water out into the cage. At the end of each week or when the bottle is about half empty, you take it down, clean it, refill it, and put it back in place.

If you notice your hamster chewing on the water bottle, it means one of three things. The bottle is empty; the bottle has somehow gotten plugged and your hamster can't get any water out; or he needs something to chew on because he is stressed. Check the water bottle, and fill it if it's empty. (Is the substrate wet? Change it!) Put in a few lengths of branches (apple, pear, or orange are particularly good, if

Be sure to provide a water bottle your hamster can reach easily. This is a cream banded Syrian.

you can find a source), some hamster chow, a dog biscuit, or hamster toys, so your hamster will have something pleasant to chew on.

Food Dish

You can buy nice ceramic or metal food dishes for your hamster, but expect the dish to serve as a way station. Hamsters tend to move the best portions of their food to their bedding, in order to make snacking more comfortable. Why get out of bed for food when all you need to do is nose around a little? This means, of course, when you clean the cage you throw a lot of food away. You simply shrug. If you have a compost pile, you can dump the shavings on the compost bed,

and if it rains you have a nice green-sprouted compost bed.

I found a combined food dispenser/toy that reminded me of the pigeon experiments, in which a pigeon is trained to peck at a lever and is rewarded by food when the correct lever is chosen. The food dispenser had three compartments, each controlled by a lever. I filled the compartments with hamster diet, sunflower seeds, and wild bird seed, and put the container into my hamster's cage. He loved it, waiting until late at night to press the levers, *clunk clunk clunk*, and moving out the food until the device was empty. He wasn't even moving the food into his bed—he just liked the device. Or maybe the noise.

Substrate, or Flooring for All

Hamsters are burrowing creatures, and your hamster needs to burrow. There's not much difference between a substrate—something that goes on the floor of the cage—and bedding, for hamsters. If you use a lightweight substrate that will temporarily hold a tunnel's shape, as do aspen shavings, your hamster can burrow through the substrate to his heart's content, and pile it up where he likes for his sleeping area.

If it's ten o'clock at night and you've just walked in the door with your new hamster, you don't have to go out and search for substrate. Torn strips of newspaper over a solid sheet of newspaper will work. A bit of warning, however—a hamster kept in a cage with newspaper substrate will

A red-eyed satin-coated Syrian explores a cage filled with paper substrate.

spend his time ripping and shredding the newspaper to fluff it up, and he'll get covered with rubbed-off news ink. Try to avoid this sort of extra mess, and depressing your hamster once he begins reading the newspapers and discovers what a messed-up place the media depicts the world to be! Provide unprinted newsprint or paper towels as soon as you can. Paper towels tend to compact quickly, but they are absorbent and easy to replace.

One of my friends pointed proudly to her cage that was half filled with shredded paper. "I bought a paper shredder, and brought home discarded copy paper from my office," she said. "I don't have to buy any substrate anymore. I can make all that I need." What she didn't realize was that most shredded copy paper is not absorbent. Not only will you and your hamster soon be looking at, and walking in (well, your hamster, anyway), a cage with liquid garbage on the floor, but the cage is going to smell as well. Even every-other-day cage changes aren't going to kill the odor, and one of the main purposes behind substrate is to absorb odor. If you shred your own paper, make sure you're using an absorbent shredded paper.

Your pet store is a good place to check out what's available in substrate. You'll see aspen shavings, aspen pellets, alfalfa pellets (also known as rabbit food), pecan pellets, ground walnut or pecan shells, shredded wheat stems, shredded hibiscus stems, recycled newspaper, coconut husk fiber,

There are two types of litter not to use. Here's why:

1. Clumping kitty liters—Hamsters are coprophagic, which means that, like rabbits, they eat a portion of their feces as part of the digestive process. (This is explained in the diet section, and it's no weirder than a cow chewing her cud.) Clay kitty litter is so drying it will cause your hamster's feet to become chapped and cracked (ow!). If ingested along with the feces or even the food, the clay lodges in the hamster's digestive system. Your hamster will die of intestinal obstruction.

2. Cedar-based shavings and litters—Knowledgeable hamster keepers don't use cedar in any form. They know that the aromatic oils—the phenols—are irritating to the hamster's respiratory system, and the hamster has no escape from these fumes. Yes, pet stores still sell cedar shavings. Just because something is for sale for use by hamsters (or rather, their owners), it doesn't mean that item is the best thing to use.

and cypress mulch, all of which will work to a greater or lesser degree. All are worth trying—but aspen shavings tend to work the best.

A big bag of aspen shavings will last a long time, if you have room to store it. (You can buy a bed for yourself that lifts up to reveal a hollowed-out box instead of a box spring if you're

pinched for storage space.) Remember that although online prices may be less expensive, you may have freight costs. Try not to surprise yourself.

The shavings can be placed in a thick enough layer to allow your pet to stay hidden while he sleeps and cunningly sneak from side to side in the cage and poke his head up to observe you when you aren't paying attention to him (and you thought you got a hamster so you could have fun watching him!).

The importance of a thick layer of shavings was demonstrated in a study done by von A. Hautzenberger in 2005. His findings disclosed Syrian hamsters should have cages with deep bedding. He suggested a depth of 1½ to 3 feet, to mimic the natural burrows of the golden hamster.

The pelleted substrates are very good at controlling odors and absorption. The only binder used for the pellets is water, so once the pellets get wet, they fall apart into sawdust. They do help keep the cage fresh, but they don't hold the shape of a burrow when a hamster has tunneled through them.

Another of the newer substrates is recycled newspaper. One brand looks like twisted bits of gray paper, and it's very odor- and moisture-absorbent. It's treated so any non-soy inks left in the pulp can't harm your hamster. It absorbs liquids quite well. It doesn't hold the shape of a burrow at all, but the hamsters seem to enjoy shoving it around.

You can make your own substrate, if the idea of controlling what your pet is exposed to appeals to you. Use white paper towels and tear them into strips about a half inch wide. (To make it easy, you can use the paper towels that tear off in half sheets, and then with scissors cut the half sheets into half-inch-wide strips.) Then you put them in a bucket of water and let them sit for half an hour until they get mushy and fragile. Take small handfuls of the mush and squeeze them as dry as you can with your hands. Then rolling them between your hands will remove even more water. Let the clumps dry, on a towel in the sun if you can or on your kitchen counter. Use the dried clumps as you would Carefresh or any other paper litter. My hamster enjoyed tearing the clumps into paper towel "fluffs" and used them to line his sand bed/toilet.

You can use newspaper the same way, to create your own low-cost Carefresh, but the newsprint comes off on everything, including your hands and fingernails, creating a grunge look that takes some scrubbing to remove.

Setting Up the Cage

When you get your caging and accessories home—or you take the cage out of your storage area—wash the cage down with a mild soap and water, and rinse and dry it. Now you're ready for setup.

Provide a sleeping area. Hamsters in the wild hollow out just a small room in their burrow to use as a sleeping area. They like to feel cozy while they sleep, so when they are in a cage, they'll try to find a corner to use, and they add something soft and shredded to "snug up" the room. Offer your hamster a small sleeping room, one large enough for the hamster to turn around in. There are numerous commercial "hide boxes" available, both disposable (paper tubes) and longer lasting forms (wicker to recycled plastic). I've used a small tin can, with one end cut out and the edges smoothed, and a small cardboard box with a hamster-sized entry hole cut into it. I've cut down empty tissue boxes and used them. I finally broke down and bought one of green recycled plastic, molded to look like a miniature tree trunk, if tree trunks ever came in a pale green. Empty toilet paper rolls or sections of empty paper towel rolls make good sleeping areas, and they are easy to get out of—the hamster just walks through them.

Don't hesitant to get creative for a sleeping box. A small terra-cotta flowerpot, turned upside down with an opening nipped out at the bottom edge with a pair of pliers (just nip out small bits at a time) works fine. A tiny finch nesting basket can be fastened to the side of the cage so it won't roll. Just make sure the house you provide is big enough for your hamster, offers some ventilation, and is easy to clean or throw away if it becomes soiled.

Your hamsters may or may not accept your sleeping box. I provided sleeping boxes of several designs, rather nice ones I thought, only to have them studiously ignored. They didn't want the wooden boxes, the cardboard boxes, or even the store-bought sleeping house, filled with brightly colored paper krinkles. The hamsters preferred to sleep in their shredded tissue heaps. This may have less to do with the quality or design of the sleeping boxes offered than the ambient temperature. I live in Florida, where a summertime room temperature of 80 degrees is an affordable goal. The close quarters of any sleeping box may have been too warm for fur-covered hamsters.

Whether or not your hamster accepts a sleeping box or remains a purist and wants only tissues, it's easy to replace only the bedding once or twice a week and change cage substrate every one or two weeks.

Easy-to-Provide Enrichment Items for Your Hamster

Pieces of fresh coconut

Plain popped popcorn

Cardboard tubes from paper toweling or toilet paper

Pieces of scrap lumber (only untreated lumber); scent some with vanilla or peppermint extract, dot others with food coloring

Nylabones (you can recycle those your dog has chewed down to nubs too small for him; disinfect first by immersion in a ten-percent bleach solution: ¼ cup bleach to 2½ cups tap water, then rinse thoroughly.

Branch sections from fruit trees

Add at least one food dish, one being for timothy hay and perhaps another for the seed mix/kibble that forms the other part of their diet. You can easily get by with one feeding dish, a combo unit, so to speak, because hamsters don't like to leave food in a feeding dish and will generally shove it out of the dish and move it elsewhere.

Hamsters enjoy exploring their cage when they awaken, and the addition of a few ramps and platforms will greatly increase the available floor space. If your cage doesn't have these built in, you can check with your local pet store for proper hamster ramps. These snap into place and are generally quite serviceable. If your local store doesn't stock ramps, you can build some using items found at your local home improvement store. I've made ramps from unfinished ¼ × 3-inch hobbyist wood strips, and from strips of ½ × 1-inch hardware cloth with the raw edges folded over. These worked well and were used by the hamsters. The metal ones had an advantage in that they couldn't get chewed up, but that's an advantage from my viewpoint only. Maybe my hamsters liked chewing up the wooden ramps; it took them the better part of a month to render the ramps unsightly, and they were quite persevering in their work. It was only a matter of twenty minutes to build some new ones. Hint: If you're going to try the wooden ramps, build a couple of extras when you're building the first, so you can replace them easily if they get chewed up. I always discovered cage

Two Syrians use the same exercise wheel, but soon they'll quit and start to fight.

renovations were needed late at night. Having a few extra ramps on hand was a real help.

Hamsters love exercise wheels. These are important to keeping any hamster busy and content. If your caging doesn't have room for an exercise wheel, rethink your caging. My Chinese hamster loved his exercise wheel so much that he moved in a bit of food, I guess to snack on when he got hungry. His cage went squeak, squeak, clatter, clatter all night. Then he pulled in some shredded bedding, maybe to make catching naps a little more comfortable, so his cage went squeak, clatter, swish until I greased the wheel with Vaseline. Then he spent the better part of twenty minutes trying to pull in an empty paper towel roll, only to fail in

the end. His wheel was quieter after that, but he seemed okay with it.

Wash out the water bottle, fill it, and suspend it from the side of the cage so the hamster can drink from a standing position. Take a moment to admire the cage; it will rarely look this neat again.

Open the cage door, or if you're using a cage where the top comes off, you may find it easier to handle everything from the top. It will be easier to put the hamster inside that way, rather than trying to cram your hamster-laden hand through the fairly small door.

Take your hamster out of his travel box (hold him firmly so he won't drop to the tabletop and run; see page 38 for advice on the three basic hamster holds), talk to him, and put him in his cage. Once he's inside, close

out of the cage, and generally having a good time.

Once your hamster has been in the cage for a day or two, you'll be able to find the area he or she has elected to use as a toilet. Make it easy to clean this area without disrupting the hamster by "installing" a removable container, sort of a litter pan. I used the bottom of an orange juice carton, trimmed off about an inch high.

To install the litter pan, remove the soiled litter from the cage, but keep a tablespoon or so of the soiled litter and put it into the litter pan. You can add clean sand or shredded paper on top. The odor will help your hammie figure out what the container is for. Every second day or so, empty the litter pan, add new sand, and put it back into place. Once your hamster has used his litter pan, it will greatly cut down on the frequency you'll need to clean the entire cage. Scoop out the bathroom area every second day or so, and add fresh substrate in that area.

Solid plastic exercise wheels squeak a lot less than the metal wheels (you'll appreciate this late at night).

the door or replace the top and take a moment to tell your hamster that he has a new cage, a new owner, and a new life. Give him a half day or so to settle down, although it may take considerably less time. Every time you go past the cage, even if your hamster is asleep, stop and talk to him for a moment or so. You want him to get used to the sound of your voice and to the idea of seeing you at regular intervals. Expect to see him regarding you gravely through the sides of his cage the first night you have him. The next day, take him out and handle him for a few minutes, and daily after that, in quarter-hour increments. You want your hamster to associate you with being petted, eating good things, being

Cleaning in General

Once a week or so, change the substrate in your hamster's cage. If you have no place to stash him, try letting him run around in your tub while his cage is being cleaned (close the drain, of course), or you can empty your tallest kitchen trash can and put him in that. Dump the substrate and his bedding. If the cage still smells, wash the tray and bottom part of the cage with soapy water, and rinse. Wash the food dishes and the water dish (if you use one), and change the water in his lab bottle. Disinfect the bottle and the sipper tube by immersing them in a ten-percent bleach solution (¼ cup bleach to 2½ cups of tap water) and rinsing them thoroughly before refilling. A quick dry with paper towels, and you can add new substrate, replace the newly filled food dishes and water source, add new bedding, and you're done. If you have a very large cage (lucky hamster!) you can scoop out the soiled areas, spot-clean the cage flooring (there are special safe cleaners you can buy for this), and replenish the substrate.

Gently scoop up your hamster, pet him for a moment, and tell him what a splendid beast he is. Put him back in his cage. You can reward him, if you like, with a bit of carrot. You may reward yourself with the rest of the carrot, or go for a more complex carbohydrate in the form of carrot cake.

Interesting enough, cleaning a hamster's cage is disrupting for the animal. Several researchers have done studies on the distressing effects of cage cleaning on hamsters, but I can't vouch for the aesthetic value of hamster caging in a lab (those cages may well be the minimum 10-inches square), other than to say the ones I've seen are extremely plain. I never noticed my hamsters exhibiting any signs of distress at being plopped back into a

The classic Campbell's hamster.

cleaned cage (except once—and the upset was caused by where I placed my hamster while I cleaned her cage—see note below). If you worry about this, you can probably reduce your worry level by changing the bedding box or loose bedding and the litter pan more frequently than you change the entire cage.

Note: Pay attention to where you stash your hamster while you clean his cage. Once when cleaning my hamster's cage, I put Maudie, my yellow-black hamster, in a tall bucket with pine shavings, the same way I always do. She curls up and goes back to sleep. Like always, I put the bucket on my kitchen table to keep my dogs from hanging their panting faces over the edge.

I heard Maudie jumping up and down in the bucket as I cleaned her cage, and she seemed agitated when I lifted her out and put her in her cleaned cage. I mentioned Maudie's agitation to my husband, Dick. He said, "Well of course, that's the bucket I used when I caught the shrew in our yard yesterday." Mind you, Maudie is many generations removed from the wild, and she has never been exposed to a shrew—until now. It's easy to deduce that she was responding to the odor of an enemy she's never met.

When you clean your hamster's cage you'll have to decide for yourself whether to scoop up and put his food stash back in the newly cleaned cage. After a few cautious sniffs, I just figured my hamster had probably already urinated on it and he was going to have to create another stash. I coldheartedly scooped out the food, the bedding, and the substrate, and replaced it with new.

Cage Enrichment

Cage enrichment is a fairly new term to describe any toy or "cage accessory" added to the cage beyond a sleeping tube, food, and water. You'd certainly be bored if you were confined to a single room with nothing to do, and hamsters are really not the stay-at-home type.

Is the work worth it? You bet—I easily found a dozen or so recent scientific journal articles about hamster cage enrichment and the benefits thereof. Those benefits include

reduced aggression, better scores on problem-solving tests, and less fear.

Researchers have very modest ideas of what enriches a cage. All I can say is I'm glad they aren't Santa Claus. One researcher used clear Mason jars and sections of PVC pipes, offering them one at a time in the cage to judge reactions more accurately (and I suppose to keep the hammies from getting too excited about their new caging arrangements). The research noted, with a faint air of surprise, that the hamsters were innovative in their use of their enrichment items—they stood on top of the jars and pipes, gnawed on them, urinated in them, and stored food in them. Juveniles slept together in them. The researchers reported that the hamsters in the control cage—without any enrichment—spent more time sleeping and eating than hamsters in the enriched cages. Enrichment seemed to increase species-specific behavior like scent marking, gnawing, hoarding, and digging. Older hamsters interacted with the enrichment objects less than the younger hamsters, and the enrichment items decreased the aggression in the younger hamsters more than in the older hamsters.

In case you're considering which excitement won out, the hamsters preferred the jars over the PVC pipes.

But you have many resources at your disposal. If you walk by the hamster or bird section at your local pet store, you'll see devices galore—levered food-dispensing containers, plastic balls with jingle bells inside,

chew blocks, chew tubes, carrot holders, dyed wooden toys (vegetable dyes only), hanging chains with balls, bells, and dowel pieces attached—the variety is limitless. Certainly you can buy whatever you think will appeal to your hamster; none of these items are particularly expensive. The added good news is that you can also provide a lot of stimulation for your hamster with items you find about your house.

You can use a box of sand. The first time I used sand, I "cooked" it in my oven for an hour at 350 degrees, in order to kill anything pathogenic. (My husband saw the oven was on, opened the door, and saw a glass dish heaped with sand. He looked puzzled, but said nothing. He did say "Let's go out for dinner" that night, so this might be worth trying again.) Once the sand

cooled, I poured it into an empty tissue box—the half-sized box—and put it in the cage. The hamsters seemed pleased. I never saw them roll or dig in it per se, but within a day they'd shoved most of the sand out of the box and had moved bedding in.

My second effort at using sand was for Humboldt, my Campbell's hamster. He got play sand, shaken through plastic window screening and shoveled into a clean ceramic dog bowl. He loved it, digging and shoveling it around with his chest and forepaws, and then he adopted the bowl as his personal toilet. I changed the sand weekly. When I replaced the gray play sand with red sand from a former reptile caging use, he moved more than half of it from the dish. He moved the sand to the corner he used for unwanted things, shoved most of it out of his cage, and covered what he could not pick up with shavings. What was left in the dish he covered with shredded tissues.

Add an empty soup can, making sure there are no rough edges. Avoid offering large paper clips or unused house keys as toys, to avoid problems with zinc toxicity. Give them sections of apple or orange branches to gnaw on. Cut paper strips and use a glue stick to make a small paper chain. Whatever route you take, remember to change the items in your hamster's cage every other week or so, just to offer him a bit of variety. But don't jam-pack his cage. You will see cages on the Internet that are loaded with every toy imaginable. I vote to give your hammie some room to walk/explore and limit the number of caging accessories.

Dealing with an Escapee

Although I like to think my own cages were escape-proof, I was proven wrong (yes, I remembered Israel Aharoni every time). One hamster scrambled atop his watering bottle and out the top of his uncovered cage. The other hamster shoved open the door of his converted birdcage. Neither escape was a success. The first hamster fell straight down into the bucket I used when changing cages (fortunately the bucket had 4 inches of fresh pine shavings, so the hamster was fine if

a bit disappointed when I found him the next morning). The other hamster darted past one of my hound dogs, whose gazelle-like vertical leap told me what was afoot—I was able to reassure my dog that the hamster was no threat to his safety, once I pulled 50 pounds of quivering hound off my shoulder. I retrieved the hamster, who was totally unafraid and more interested in watching the dog than keeping his freedom. I put him back in his cage and added a clip to the door.

But most hamster owners aren't that lucky. They find the cage door open and the hamster is nowhere in sight. You can look for him—you can move the furniture around, noting at the same time the quantities of dust bunnies that live underneath and

behind furniture—but you may not see him. Or if you see him, you may not be able to grab him before he dashes off. One friend's hamster found his way into a bathroom and set up his new home underneath the floor of the sink cupboard. My sister's hamster found happiness underneath a refrigerator. Still another hamster crawled up, inside a sofa. All the hiding places offered space (bigger than the cage, eh?), darkness, and privacy.

You may be able to borrow a rodent live trap, called HavaHart traps, from your humane society, exterminator, or your local animal shelter—these are rectangular wire boxes with trip doors at each end that close when the food on the trip tray inside is disturbed. You can make your own live trap with an empty tin can, a mouse trap, and a piece of hardware cloth.

You may be able to rig a trap with the old bucket-and-food trick. You stand the highest bucket (or trash can) in the middle of the floor and put shavings for padding and something yummy and smelly in the bottom—perhaps hamster seed mix, some apple pieces, and a little peanut butter. You stack a staircase of books to the top of the bucket on one side. You turn off the lights, leave the room, and go to bed. With luck, the next morning (or maybe the morning after that) you look inside the bucket and there is your hamster, surrounded by shredded tissues and wearing a guilty look and traces of peanut butter around his mouth.

Hamster-proofing

Hamsters can become family pets and can be allowed to wander the house when you're home, but with a few restrictions. If you decided you want to give li'l Hammie the freedom to roam around a particular room, hamster-proof the room. Put any dogs or cats in another room and close that door, plug up the tempting holes that are hamster-sized, cover the electric cords, and move any wooden or papier-mâché sculptures you may have resting on the floor. Hamsters taste things to help identify them; if the item in question is food, that's good, if not, the hamster moves on.

I hamster-proofed the room I use for an office. For me, this simply meant taking the stuff off the floor of the closet and putting it on the shelves. I moved all the furniture—the file cabinets, the computer desk, the table—about 4 inches away from the wall so li'l Hammie could get behind them and I could peer around *them* to see *him*. After I moved the furniture out, I hastily vacuumed, so Hammie wouldn't get dusty wandering around. Since there are no foodstuffs in the room, well, none that aren't eaten immediately, I didn't have to hamster-proof any food containers, if indeed it's possible to protect foodstuffs against a determined set of gnawing teeth. I moved heavy books from the bottom shelf of my printer stand to a higher shelf, so Hammie couldn't get squashed by a large tome. I covered some electrical cords with split lengths of half-inch

aquarium tubing (about a dollar a foot at an aquarium store), and sprayed the others with Bitter Apple, to discourage nibbling. Lastly, I told my entire family that Hammie had roaming privileges in my room and they'd need to watch their feet when they came into the room.

Once the room was ready, I waited until evening. I put Hammie's cage on the floor, surrounded the area in front of the doorway with assorted hamster toys, and opened the door. It took him awhile to get his entire body out of the cage doorway (I'm sure my room seemed very large to a creature accustomed to the confines of his cage). But Hammie did venture forth and ran directly behind a file cabinet. It took

him the better part of a week of daily forays before he seemed eager to come out and explore when I opened the cage door. Getting him back inside his cage took some time. It took bribery (a raisin trail leading to the cage) to get him back in his cage.

He's only allowed out while I'm there, but he's busy while he's out. Because he took an inordinate interest in the carpet in one corner of the room, I had to cover the spot with books to get him to stop trying to dig down through it. Once a week or so, I remove the stash of seeds and nuts he's placed under the printer stand.

Hammie does seem to enjoy his time out of the cage, and he peers at me from around corners as I work.

Chapter Five
Diet

Pet hamsters are among the easiest small animals to feed. The easiest thing to do is to buy the best commercial hamster food you can find and augment on occasion with bits and pieces of fresh fruits, fresh veggies, and an occasional mealworm or cricket or two. What you need to look for is a diet that will provide your hamster with 12–15 percent protein and 3–6 perfect fat.

The hamster foods fall roughly into two types. There are chow diets, where all the ingredients are ground up, mixed together, and compacted into uniform brown squares with all the visual appeal of cardboard. Although this diet may not seem appealing, it is a complete diet and provides gnawing exercise for your hamster as well. Chows (also called pelleted foods) are your best choice because your hamster can't pick and choose what he eats. It will probably come as no surprise to you that many animals want to eat foods that they like, not just foods that are good for them.

The other type of hamster food consists of mixed seeds and ground grains. The mixed-seed manufacturers' slant on mixed-seed diets is that mixes are better for hamsters than chows because the mixed-seed diets

provide activity opportunities hamsters will snoop around in their dish of mixed seeds.

This is in effect "foraging," just as a hamster would do in the wild, without of course the long walks between seeds. The hamster that finds in the wild what's put into seed mixes is one lucky hamster, that's for sure. One is tempted to say, on reading the ingredients list, "Oh, I could live on that. It's just a fortified type of loose granola." One mix includes, in addition to the usual list, almonds, dehydrated apple, and dried carrots, banana, and papaya. No wonder most hamster *owners* like the seed mixes!

But the sad truth is, some items in the mixes aren't all that good for hamsters. A diet based on sunflower seeds leads to obesity and a calcium deficit, which leads to weakened bones, hardly what your little explorer needs. Peanuts are very high in protein but can lead to dietary upsets and coat changes. Sweets, in the form of dried fruits or molasses-tinged seed mixes, can lead to cavities, resulting in loss of teeth and root abscesses (as evidenced by salivation, face swelling, and loss of appetite). Hamsters need their teeth.

One food most people won't think of is hay, either timothy or alfalfa, or a mix of the two. Hamsters in the wild are grass-eaters; they eat it in the field and they pack it into their cheeks and they take it home and stash it in their larders until winter comes. Grass helps keep their teeth worn down. It's easy to add this component to your hamster's diet, either by buying hay or by pulling fresh grass, if you have access to grass that you know hasn't been treated with a pesticide or herbicide. You can buy packaged hay, either in bread-loaf-sized bags or compressed into brownie-sized cubes, at your pet store.

No matter which diet you decide to offer your pet, read the label before you buy. Some diets, both the pel-

A platinum Campbell's tries a seed mix—and eats the seeds she likes.

let and the seed mixes, have added a sweetener to the food. I was surprised to find that I was feeding my hamsters cane molasses with every scoop of seed mix I put into the cages.

While you're reading labels, check to see if the food should be refrigerated once it's been opened; some brands will advise this. Even if the food doesn't have to be chilled, buy in quantities that you'll use up within three months or so. You want to feed your hamster food you know is fairly fresh, and if you've ever opened a container of bird seed that's been on your shelf for some time and found that tiny moths have emerged from the mix, you know that "fresh" includes the concept "bug-free." You might see references online about the high oil content of some diets and how this could cause the foods to deteriorate if not refrigerated. Although I've never had any hamster food go rancid because it was too old, I've never had any on hand for more than three months. (One particularly short-lived seed mix delighted my dogs. They nosed off the cover of the container and were industriously lapping up the contents when I found them. They seemed to enjoy the food, and I'll bet the molasses enhancement was a factor.)

And remember, all hamsters need access to fresh water all the time.

Vitamin and Mineral Supplements

When you discuss food, you can't help but get into a discussion about vitamin supplements. Most adult humans take vitamins, as a preventative measure. Commercial hamster diets are complete diets, we are told, but at the same time those same food manufacturers produce and sell vitamin supplements. What's going on — are the manufacturers just pulling a fast one?

Most hamster keepers depend on a varied diet and do not offer vitamins. But if you want to be very careful about what you provide your hamster, you could look upon a vitamin supplement as a form of insurance. If you feed a seed mix, your hamsters may pick and choose what they eat. It is possible that a vitamin supplement will help fill in when a hamster's base diet is inadequate.

Vitamins come in either liquid or solid (powder) form, designed to be added to the food or to the water in the water bottle. If you're worried about your hamster refusing to drink because he doesn't like the way the vitamins taste, you may want to add a second water bottle and put the drops in that bottle only.

Interestingly enough, researchers admit that even after all these years, not much is known about the mineral requirements of hamsters. Nonetheless, there are mineral supplements for hamsters on the market. One of the newer items is a calcium tablet that's flavored with cricket bits. That may sound ghoulish, but if you've ever offered your hamster a live cricket, you've seen a hamster make a fool of himself, leaping upon and crunching down on the insect before you finish saying, "I don't think he's going to eat that, ohhhhhh, *yuck*." These supplements give your hamster calcium, a necessary mineral, with the tantalizing taste of an actual insect. And you don't have to look at, buy, chase down, or hold a single insect.

Make your own mix: C. H. Keeling, a hamster fancier and breeder in England, made his own hamster diet from bran, crushed oats, and soya meal, to which he stirred in a standard hamster mix that contained bits of rat blocks, sunflower seed, dried corn, pea meal, corn flakes, dried peas, and wild bird seed. Keeling added fresh foods to this admittedly dry diet, varying among apple slices, carrots, and cabbage (which his hamsters only nibbled on). His Chinese hamster families enjoyed as a group (or chose to ignore) grass, dandelions, cherries, grapes, and peas.

The big pitfall with creating your own food is that unless you work at the numbers for protein, fat, fiber, mineral, and vitamin content, you're feeding your hamster food that may not provide what he needs. You may also end up with a bucket of your private mix that your hamster will never finish before it goes buggy. I found it easier to read and compare labels and buy the commercial mixes.

How much can your hamster eat? A Syrian needs, on the average, about a tablespoon of food (10 gms) a day, plus a few supplements like bits of carrot, apple, or a 1-inch length of celery. Offer *at least* the same amount to a Chinese, a Campbell's, a winter white, or Roborovski, because these hamsters seem to have a higher metabolism than the Syrians.

Fresh foods can include almost any sort of fruit or vegetable. The only ones to be wary of are the leafy greens, like romaine or spinach. Giving a piece larger than an inch square can cause temporary diarrhea.

Snacks

You might be amazed at the variety and number of hamster snacks available for you and your hammie. Use them cautiously, because most are essentially candy and are very appealingly packaged, using bright colors like red, which is an appetite stimulant in humans. Some of them look a lot like human food. I was curious about some snacks that looked like brightly colored sticks, and tasted them. They were sweet, so I checked the label. The main ingredients were flour and corn syrup, not much to offer nutrition-wise.

The snack products fall into two basic groups: the mixes and the single-item foods. The mixes combine things like peanuts, molasses, papaya, apples, carrots, and sunflower seeds, usually compressed into nuggets large enough for a human to easily handle.

The single-food treats are generally a dried fruit or vegetable. The small ears of dried corn look like they'd be fun as well as providing hours of disassembly time. Another manufacturer offers dried mango, papaya, banana, and pineapple.

Making Your Own Snacks

If the sugar content of the snack "biscuits" bothers you, you can make your own. This recipe was modified from one at *hamstersinfo101.com*.

Set your oven at 350°F.

2/3 c. whole-wheat flour
3 T. sugar-free peanut butter (chunky or smooth)
1/3 c. crushed dog biscuit
1/3 c. oatmeal
about 5 T. water (add this as needed, starting with 3 T.)

Work the ingredients together with your hands to create a thick paste, like a cookie dough but not as sticky. You can shape the dough any way you like for baking, but here's what worked

Fresh Foods for Your Hamster

Acorns	Green beans
Apples	Kale
Broccoli	Peas
Cabbage	Spinach
Carrots	Sweet potato
Cauliflower	Turnip
Celery	Watercress
Corn	Zucchini
Cucumbers	
Dandelions	
(unsprayed	
leaves and	
flowers)	

best for me: Take about a 1-cup portion of the dough and press it into a long block, about an inch or so wide and 4 inches long, on a corner of a sheet of parchment paper the size of your cookie sheet. Add another piece of parchment paper on top and use a rolling pin to create a treat block about a half-inch thick, keeping the rectangle shape. Take off the top piece of parchment and use a knife to deeply score the block across its length and width into ½-inch squares. Repeat this shaping with the rest of the dough on the other quads of the parchment paper, and place the sheet onto a cookie sheet. Bake for 25 minutes, or until the dough blocks sound hollow when tapped. Remove the cookie sheet from the oven and let it cool for about 5 minutes. While the blocks are still warm, use a knife to cut the scored blocks into ¼-inch mini-blocks. Once the mini-treats have cooled completely,

store in an airtight container in your refrigerator. Whatever your hamsters don't eat, your dogs will.

Are snacks necessary? No, not at all, even though you may enjoy feeding your pet something you know he likes. You need to keep his nutrition in mind. Hamsters will willingly eat more sweet treats than a balanced diet, so you'll have to limit the treats offered.

If You're Leaving Home

The ability to store food is one reason why you can leave your hamster for three or four days without worrying. Give him fresh water, make certain his cage has just been cleaned, and check his seed/food supply (and top it off, if needed). If you're worried about sudden temperature changes in your house or apartment, the cage is a self-contained unit that can be handed to a friend or neighbor.

Your hamster will snack along with you when you prepare dinner.

Chapter Six
Hamster Communication

Hamsters can communicate quite well with each other, using scent, body posture, and sounds. We puny humans are pretty much limited to interpreting a few of the postures and some of their sounds (hamster scent, thank goodness, is a closed book to us), but even a partial knowledge of postures and sounds will help you understand what's going on in your hamster's world. You'll learn even more if you place your hamster's cage where you can watch him. I put my hamster cages on a table next to my desk so I could keep an eye on them and their actions.

Let's talk first about body language. Often this doesn't need any words to complete the message. You may remember returning home late one night and finding your parent waiting, hands on hips. Not a word is spoken, but you know you're in trouble, and subsequent penalties only reinforce this initial interpretation.

Here are a few ways your hamster uses body language to tell you how he's feeling or what he's thinking. In many cases, body language is a clue to a high stress level, not a good state for a hamster. As you get to know your hamster, you'll be able to see if he's calm and relaxed or if he's stressed,

and you can govern your actions accordingly.

- Hamster watches you with ears erect: He's curious about something but pretty calm. I looked up from my desk to find Amelia, my Syrian, sitting on her haunches with her ears erect and just watching *me*. I responded with a bit of carrot.
- Hamster's ears are laid back: Your hamster is suspicious of something and is watching you carefully, or perhaps your dog has stuck his inquisitive nose near the cage too many times. Your hamster's next reaction is to try a quick nip.
- Ears forward, cheek pouches puffed up: Your hamster is feeling frightened. Being purchased from the pet store is very stressful on hamsters—they will run around their pet store cage if they are quick enough, ears forward, but they can't get away.
- Hamster grooms self: The hamster seeks to reassure itself that everything is fine after being moved, perhaps after a cage cleaning. If the hamster has just awakened, self-grooming helps him get ready for a spin on his wheel or for a quick check of the food dish for something new and tasty.

• Hamster stretches: There are two meanings to this movement, both dependent on circumstances. Head position is the key. A hamster will stretch when he's feeling relaxed. If you are holding your hamster and he stretches with his head up and back, ears relaxed, accept it as a compliment that he likes you and is comfortable in your hands. A hamster will also stretch out and hold the position but keep his face level and his ears in the alert mode. This hamster is checking out a new situation or the presence of another hamster within scent range—he's doing a risk assessment, trying to figure out what sort of trouble, if any, he's in. He's not upset, he's just being careful. Does stretching make a hamster look larger, and is size a factor in hamster-to-hamster communication? Perhaps.

Body pressed to the ground, this Roborovski hamster tries to figure out if any other hamster has been around lately.

• Cheek pouches hastily emptied: Your hamster may feel insecure, as if he may need to flee. When I brought my just-purchased Campbell's hamster home from the pet store and placed him in his new cage, he used his hind feet to hurriedly empty his cheek pouches. I thought at the time he was "marking" his new home—now I know he was stressed out and ready to take possible action against any intruder, meaning me.

• Hamster stands on back feet and moves front arms together, almost as if he's boxing: Your hamster feels threatened and is countering with aggression. When I opened the big cage door to my Campbell's hamster's cage just after I brought him home, he bravely stood up and balled his tiny fists, with his cheeks puffed out (easy to do, since they were empty).

• Teeth chatter: This is a high-pitched sound of short duration. Your hamster is trying to forestall aggression by an intruder (you) by saying, "Back off!"

• Hamster is startled and leaps away when you approach cage: You're literally moving too fast. Your hamster isn't feeling safe and could use some time by himself before you approach him again. A hamster will hurl himself out of your hands when you pick him up if you aren't careful. When I held a hamster at my pet store, he launched himself out of my cupped hands like a flying squirrel. He landed with a thump and with no obvious damage, but this is not a good way to get acquainted.

• Hamster flops onto back and displays teeth: This is one way the loser in a hamster fight signals defeat. Your hamster is saying you are the winner. Respect/acknowledge his action by backing off.

• Hamster creeps along floor of cage, especially near the walls: He feels uncertain and just a bit frightened. This behavior is typical of a hamster placed into a new cage. He is doing a little recon of the area. He'll explore the center of the cage once the perimeter is secured.

• Hamster burrows through clean litter in his cage: He's happy and checking to see if perhaps there might be some delicious things to eat hidden away.

Hamster "Speech"

You've heard your hamsters squeak as they wander about their cage, and you've certainly heard Syrians vocalize if placed together, just before they fight. Your own hamster may squeak when you first try to pick him up. Infant hamsters that are too cold have a special vocalization they make, designed to elicit maternal care from an adult, but this call can be entirely ultrasonic or partially sonic. What we know now is that many hamster calls or vocalizations are ultrasonic.

Adults produce short calls, lasting just 6-to-17 one-hundredths of a second. These calls are so short even someone with very good hearing won't pick up on them. A research lab can record the calls and analyze the pitch and modulation. Subsequent hamster reactions to the calls indicate the calls are sexually oriented, to attract a mate and to instigate mating behavior. The calls are closely linked to chemical messages that elicit sexual behavior.

Females call when they are receptive to mating, and interestingly enough, these calls are loud enough to be heard from a distance of 30 feet. Both male and female hamsters will call when they see or smell a hamster of the opposite sex, but these calls are ultrasonic.

If the idea of listening to your hamster intrigues you, you can get more information on ultrasonic recording and conversion from the U.S.-based Bat Conservation Society, or the Wildlife Recording Society or Wildlife Acoustics Company, both in the U.K.

Hamster-to-Hamster Interaction

Most hamster-to-hamster interactions deal with aggression or sexual messages. A hamster's highest priority is to survive, and finding a way to deal with another hamster either as an enemy or as a potential mate, is a primo survival strategy. Robert E. Johnson at Cornell University is one of the researchers who has shared his observations of hamster postural, auditory, and chemical communication. It's a pretty sophisticated system, even if the messages are limited. Here are the

One Syrian sniffing another is usually a prelude to fighting.

follow are appropriate to that information. Hamsters that are related sniff-ID each other for a shorter time than unrelated hamsters, sort of "Oh. It's you." A male that has been bested by another male in a fight will sniff-ID that male and display tension/dismay in his body posture, with his ears very upright, his mouth partially open, and his body leaning back from the other male. The subordinate male will then turn and depart. A female in estrous will sniff-ID and turn to display what is tactfully described as a solicitation walk and assume the lordosis position, which tells the male that she's interested in immediate mating. (When you don't have a big vocabulary, there's no sense in mincing words.)

The Circle 'n' Sniff: The two hamsters act like two strange dogs checking each other out, circling each other, but they alternate positions in a "T" arrangement. The hamster that's the upright of the "T" sniffs the mid-regions of the other hamster (dwarf hamsters have another scent gland on the belly, just above the navel). The hamster currently sniffing may actually jam his or her head under the body of the other hamster, almost as if in an effort to topple the other hamster from its feet or in order to bite the underside. The hamsters shift positions and continue to circle while they decide which hamster will be dominant. The dominate position is the upright of the T, the hamster with his head under the body of the first hamster. The subordinate hamster may sit back on his haunches

actions and what they mean. (If you've never seen any of these actions happen, don't be surprised. Johnson and his lab staff have spent a lot of time watching, taking videos, and analyzing these movements. (If you ever find Mr. Johnson sitting next to you on a plane, please thank him for this work.)

Physical Communication

The Approach: Hamsters approach each other and lean toward each other, sniffing. They sniff-inspect each other's muzzle, from the edge of the nose to the base of the ear (there's a scent gland on the bottom edge of the ear). The gesture reminds me of two human females, forced into a social situation and kissing the air beside each other's face and trying not to wrinkle their noses in distaste.

What hamsters learn from this action evidently tells them the sex and perhaps the individual identity of the other hamster, since the actions that

in a more or less upright position to avoid being thrown off balance, which leads to another classic position, the Face-to-Face Sparring.

Face-to-Face Sparring: The aggressor here tries to bite the subordinate's belly while the subordinate remains upright and tries to push away the aggressor. Positions tend to shift rapidly. Although it can be difficult to see who is the aggressor and who is the subordinate during these encounters, the subordinate is the one sitting more upright, with the arms and paws extended, the digits splayed, and the mouth open. No audible signals are evident, other than some squeaking. Subordinates move in a jerky, motion-picture frame-by-frame motion, while the dominant males move quickly and smoothly.

Appeasement: Chimpanzees and gorillas use an appeasement gesture of one extended hand, eyes averted. Humans raise one hand to shoulder level, elbow bent, palm facing out, and avert their eyes, when trying to avoid a fight or disagreement. Hamsters use much the same gesture, especially when approached from the side by another hamster. The approached hamster seeks to avoid a confrontation as it holds out one paw, fingers splayed, palm down.

Hamsters on the losing end of a fight or that don't wish to fight use a second gesture of appeasement, the Tail Flick. The animal will freeze in place, back arched upward and tail upright. If the winner of the fight is a male, he will briefly mount the loser. If the winner is a female, she won't bother. In any case, the tail flick indicates that the hamster doesn't want to fight anymore.

Sometimes appeasement doesn't work, and the fight escalates to a series of motions Johnson calls Rolling Fighting.

Rolling Fighting: The aggressor may be standing upright or on all fours, as he/she launches an attack toward another hamster. The aggressing hamster endeavors to bite the other hamster's midsection, where the light-colored belly fur meets the darker fur of the back. The two hamsters curve

Two Syrians begin a fight by pushing with their hands.

their bodies around each other's mid-sections and become a rolling, biting, furball. The action halts and may end if one of the hamsters freezes in a belly-up position, a surrender signal. The loser then tries to leave and will career around the cage trying to find a way out. In the wild, that hamster will escape the aggressor. In a cage, he's stuck.

Sometimes the dominate hamster isn't through and will follow to continue the attack and can seriously injure or kill the loser. There is where intervention needs to take place in the form of a few squirts from a water bottle and one of the hamsters being removed from the cage. And there are lasting effects from social defeat, at least for the loser. Syrian hamsters deal with social defeat by increasing their food intake with a concomitant increase in body and fat mass. I've know humans who've done the same thing.

The Role of Scent

Hamsters leave chemical messages via scent glands, which vary in location and number depending on the hamster species.

The Syrian and the Roborovski hamsters have paired flank scent glands, one high on each hip. The hip glands are visible on the unfurred young but are soon hidden by the growing fur. The flank glands of the males are almost twice the size of the females and secrete pheromones (scented hormones that are used in signaling members of the opposite sex). Flank glands are used to mark territory. Hamsters rub the sides of the body against vertical surfaces in their caging, much like a dog will scoot his body along a wall after he's rolled in mud. Scent from the flank glands is probably also deposited on the floor of the cage, since hamsters scratch their flanks with their hind paws.

Flank marking occurs both in nonsocial and social contexts. Nonsocial contexts may be as the hamsters enter or leave their nest area or before or after grooming. Social contexts are more intense, when they smell other hamsters of the same species or are put into contact with them. Like bears, male hamsters are stirred to mark their territory when they discover the marking of another male hamster. Syrians can detect scent markings made by their siblings or half siblings, even if those siblings were raised by different parents, and they do not react to these markings. But should the marking be made by an unrelated hamster, the Syrian begins to immediately react, actively sniffing the markings and the surrounding area.

Flank marking is also a status and agonistic (= antagonistic) indicator. Dominant hamsters mark more frequently than subordinate hamsters, even in same-sex pairings or same-sex quads. In a study of paired males, the subordinate male marked very rarely, and then it was in or adjacent to his nest, as if to protect/mark it against intrusion.

When a male is exposed to a female that is ready to breed he stops marking his turf with his scent. Females that are ready to breed stop their own marking cycle when they encounter odors from males. This reduction in marking of both sexes when sex appears imminent indicates that marking is an aggressive gesture. The priority seems to swing to making love, not war.

Researchers have actually pinpointed the scent that the male Syrian hamster finds attractive in females. The scent is a chemical compound called dimethyl disulfide, the same compound that gives the Titan Arum lily its distinctive garlicky–rotten meat scent. Of course, the concentration is much higher in the Arum lily.

A male without the ability to smell anything is indifferent to female hamsters.

Other Scent Glands

The dwarf hamsters, the Campbell's hamster and the winter white hamster, have six pairs of scent glands, located on the ears, the belly, and the genitals. Campbell's have a specialized scent gland on the belly, just anterior to the naval. Males can be seen to touch the floor of their cages with their bellies, as if marking, and female hamsters mark their area by pressing their genitals against the floor of the cage with the tail upraised.

The male winter white's ventral scent gland has been found to contain forty eight different compounds. The same gland in the female doesn't contain enough secretions for analysis; this indicates the gland has a definite sexual identification function.

Hamsters' ear glands are on the bottom side of the external ear. Females' ear glands are smaller than the males'. Males spend more time sniffing at the females' ear gland scent than at the scent from male ear glands.

The Harderian glands behind the eye secrete a liquid through the tear ducts. The glands assist in eye lubrication, photoreception (detection of light), maintenance of coat, and body temperature regulation. The glands are involved with regulating the hamster's night and day cycles. In gerbils, secretions from the Harderian glands are spread about the face during grooming. It would seem likely that the same occurs in hamsters and it is partially the Harderian and ear gland scent that hamsters are sniffing when they identify another hamster in facial sniffing.

A curious Syrian hamster moves cautiously with his ears perked forward.

Chapter Seven

Getting to Know Your Hamster

Taming Your Hamster

So there he is, in his cage. It's evening, or maybe just late afternoon, and there you are, looking at your hamster, knowing you ought to pick him up and begin taming him because you don't want to get bitten. But ummmmmmm . . . Is he tame?

Hamsters are nice creatures, even when new captives. They may be scared or very shy, but these are nice animals. Mike Murphy, the grad student who brought new Syrian stock back from Aleppo in 1971, was amazed at how quickly the hamsters he and his wife captured tamed down—and these were "wild" hamsters.

The 1930s Syrian descendants have been bred for disposition for many years. Breeders and researchers don't like getting bitten any more than you and I do. Pet hamsters—all of them—have been and are being bred for disposition. All you need is a bit of your time to work with your hamster, so he'll know you aren't bad news.

So stop worrying. Wash your hands, and dry them (you don't want your hamster to think you smell like a ripe tomato or something else tasty). Open the cage and look at your hamster.

If he's sleeping, rustle the substrate near him until he wakes up, or very gently jiggle the cage. Hamsters don't like to be awakened suddenly, because it might mean something is going to eat them. It's much like standing next to your dad's bed early on a Saturday morning and announcing, "Some guys at the door say they are from the IRS. They say they want to talk to you." That's not a good way to wake up.

Waking up needs to be a pleasant experience for all concerned. So always give your hamster a moment to wake up. He needs to open his shoe-button eyes and focus on your earnest face (that ought to wake him up). Put a few sunflower seeds in the palm of your hand, and put your hand in his cage so he can see the seeds. Keep your hand in place for a few minutes while he builds up his courage to approach it. Let him grab a seed or two and scurry off before you take your hand out. Talk to him so he'll learn the sound of your voice. (Don't slip the sunflower seeds through the bars of the cage or through the top—hammies need to associate wonderful things with your actual hand. You need to circumvent their typical territoriality so nipping never occurs to them.)

Repeat this once or twice an evening for a few days, so he will realize you're a friend. Once he sits on your hand to crack the first sunflower seeds, you can begin to teach him about being picked up (and if you are more comfortable wearing a thin pair of gloves, do so).

Your hamster will soon associate your hands with wonderful things.

Open the cage door as you always do. Once he's looking at you, reach in and scoop him up in your fingers (from his rump side first is best). Close your fingers around him. As soon as you get your hand off the substrate, cup your other hand under him to make a cage of your fingers. Talk to him while you do this. Of course he won't be able to understand your words, but he'll be able to pick up on the tone you use.

Hold him closely so he can't escape, or cup him against your body. You would be better off if you were close to the floor or on a bed so if he blasts out of your hands, he won't be hurt. He needs to feel secure, like he's not going to be dropped. You don't want to drop him, ever, because a fall for something this small can injure him.

If you are still hesitant to simply reach in and hold him, put his cage on your bed, and create a barricade around the cage and you with boxes or bedding. Sit on the bed with the cage. Open the cage and let him come out to explore. Use the back of your hand to gently stroke his back, keeping your fingers away from his mouth. Scoop him up in your hands, lift for just a moment, and put him back down again, opening your hands so he isn't restrained. You could even do this same "gentle scoop and briefly lift" when he's in his cage, just moving him a trifle before opening your hands and putting him down.

But what if your hamster sees you coming, rolls over on his back, bares his teeth, and squeaks? Back off. Go back to hand-feeding him tasty treats for a few minutes. The little guy is scared, and he's trying to fend off what he sees as your attack. Talk to him, and try to gently stroke his back.

Try the hand scoop again, or shoo him into an empty tin can and tilt it upright so he can't launch himself into space. If he's sought shelter in his empty paper towel roll, pick up the roll and cover both ends. Tilt the can or uncover the lower end of the paper roll and tip him out into your hand. Hold him close to your body for just a moment, and then gently put him back in his cage. It isn't his fault he's frightened. Put yourself in his place. You're really huge, and you don't smell like a hamster.

As your hamster becomes accustomed to being in your hands, try stroking his head or back gently as you hold him. Offer him a sunflower seed or a raisin (raisin bread is a fine source of an occasional raisin).

Your hamster will enjoy being held once he gets over being frightened, but it will take several sessions before he figures out that you're his friend and not his worst enemy. With gentle overtures and gentle handling, he'll look forward to his times out of the cage with you.

Stress and Your Hamster

For being such sturdy creatures, hamsters are laid low by stress. If there

Longhair Syrians seem particularly prone to stress-induced wet-tail, which may appear just a few days after purchase.

is anything that will make your hamster's life miserable, it is stress.

Stress is when you're bothered by something, but you can't do anything about it. For a kid, it's being bullied at school and your dad telling you to "man up." For an adult, it's driving into heavy snow near a mountain pass, and it's night and you don't have snow tires on your car, and your car keeps sliding when you go around corners. For a hamster, it's being transported, being crowded in a cage, having a cage in a noisy area, being exposed to continuous bright lights, or being trapped in a corner of a cage while small hands keep trying to grab you. When you're small, even "small" things matter.

Stress is exhausting. Keyed up to fight when there is nothing obvious to fight, systems in the body break down. Wounds that would otherwise be insignificant take longer to heal. The intestinal flora balance in the small intestine is overwhelmed by a bacteria called *Lawsonia intracellularis*, and a galloping diarrhea leads to wet-tail.

Stressors that are social—such as being the loser in a fight or being crowded in a cage—don't have to be prolonged to produce marked effects on subsequent behavior. Stress can lead to depression. Anyone who has been out of work knows all about stress and depression. A depressed hamster is inactive. He avoids contact with the outside world, may eat very little (with resultant intestinal problems/diarrhea), or he may pack on the grams by overeating, selecting foods that are high in fat.

Your job is to help your hamster avoid being stressed. You need to provide caging large enough for him to select what spot he wishes to be in; clean well-ventilated caging placed in a quiet spot with a place to "hide away" during sleep; and a diet to which he is accustomed and without any moldy or insect-riddled seeds; and access to clean fresh water at all times.

In return, you will have a furry friend that will look forward to being taken out of his cage on an evening and given a treat, allowed to explore the inside of your shirt cuff, or given time to explore his own playground.

Hamsters and Other Pets

Hamsters are regarded as prey animals by larger carnivores like cats and dogs. Although you may read of curious animal alliances on the Web or in a video on YouTube, it is unrealistic and unfair to even expose your hamster to a potential carnivore. Avoid stressing your small friend. His life is already short enough.

About Breeding in General, or Simply Avoid It

On the surface, breeding your hamsters seems like an easy way to make a little money. Pet stores sell the little guys for $5 and up; if each litter is eight babies, that's $40 if you sell them yourself, $20 if you sell them to the pet store.

It doesn't quite work that way. National pet store chains won't buy from you, and they won't take your babies even if they are free. Notices in Craigslist may sell one or two babies, and you'll receive queries from those who want free hamsters to feed to snakes. Notices thumb-tacked onto bulletin boards at feed stores—if you can find a feed store—don't get much response. Even if you do sell one pup, be prepared to be asked to take it after it bites someone! (People just don't know how to handle hamsters.)

Even trying to breed specific colors can result in disaster, hamster-sized. If you have mottled Campbell's hamsters with the ruby-eyed gene, don't breed them together. The young are smaller and white—very pretty—but are evidently eyeless (anophthalmic) and may be toothless. It's a little hard to tell on the latter, because the babies die when they're two to three weeks old.

Some Syrians also carry the gene for eyelessness. Syrians that are roan in coloration or have a white belly may be heterozygous for the anophthalmic gene, meaning they have one dominant gene or gene grouping for normal coloration and normal eyes, and a recessive gene/gene grouping for the white color and eyelessness. When two of these hamsters are bred, some of the young receive both recessive genes, and as a result are white (which is why all-white hamsters merit your close examination before you buy them) and eyeless. These babies can

muddle around their cages and find food and water, but they don't have much appeal as a pet.

She Was Pregnant When I Got Her!

Yes, it happens. You get a hamster from a source that shall remain unnamed, and gosh, she's a chubby little thing. One day you awaken, stretch, and get out of bed, and as you walk past the cage, you hear squeaking, little tiny squeaks, not adult-sized. The female is hidden in her bedding, and she doesn't respond to your voice. Looks like—nope, make that *sounds* like, you have babies. Don't worry, the

Young hamsters' ultrasonic calls will summon adult attention.

Look at the ears and the snout-forward pose—young hamsters are suspicious and ill at ease.

momma hamster only needs food and water, she can take care of her babies.

Reproduction in hamsters has been so well studied and analyzed that researchers can point to hormone level changes in a blood profile and say, "It's at this point, with the estrogen levels rising, that the female becomes maternal and will choose to feed and care for her young."

When the young are most dependent on the mother's care she spends her time licking them, constructing/ fluffing up the nest, nursing, and hauling back the tiny pups who decide to check out the world outside the nest: "You there, pup number 10, get back in here, on the double!" and then sighing, "Oh, well," and bounding out of the nest, some babies still nursing,

grabbing the adventurous pup by its head and hauling him back into the nest. (As a matter of interest and as a plea for more natural nesting sites, those pups raised in a modified burrow setup as opposed to a wire cage tended to wander away from the nest less than those in a wire cage.)

As the pups get older and need a bit less of this almost-fussy tending, the activity displayed by the female parent declines, along with her estrogen levels. (If you fool her by replacing her maturing pup with younger pups that still need the massive amounts of tending, her parental behavior will be prolonged.)

As the young become more independent, the mother's involvement with her young decreases. For brief periods, she moves about the cage and climbs onto objects, sniffs the environs, grooms herself, stands up on her hind legs—almost as if she didn't have a half-dozen or more hungry mouths back in the nest. For first-time mothers, this urge to get out and look around shows a marked increase fifteen days after the birth of her young, and for mothers of multiple litters, it occurs on day 18.

If the pups are removed for a short time and then put back in the nest, as the mother's estrogen level begins to decline, the mother will exhibit what researchers call "deficiencies in maternal responsiveness," and those pups better grow up fast.

Pup Development

Hamsters are groomers. Syrian hamsters begin grooming themselves by the second week of life, moving their forepaws over the snout without touching it. By the second week, they begin licking their forepaws and brushing about the head and the snout, almost as if saying to each other, "Does my face fuzz look better fluffed this way or all forward?" At fifteen days old the pups begin coordinated licking and brushing of the entire body. No matter what the species of hamster, the head and snout grooming appears about the same time the young begin nibbling at solid food, and the whole body brushing occurs when the young begin to venture out of the nest area and begin to eliminate urine and feces without the mother's stimulation. (All these figures are from ham-

sters observed in captivity, not from the wild.)

Pups huddle with each other, move around with each other, and eat together. They also begin play fighting. Huddling is especially important while the pups are young, so everyone stays warm (very young mammals aren't very good at moderating their body temperature). When the dam or mother leaves the nest in the fourth or fifth week postpartum, the pups themselves begin to seek their own independent nest sites. The mother may move to another corner of the cage for her new nest, and again to another site. The abandoned nests are effectively dismantled by the pups as they enter and leave the nest, and steal portions of it for their own nests.

Let your hamster have some fun when you're away. Sheets of compressed cotton take a bit of chewing before they can be fluffed up.

Chapter Eight
Hamster Health

With good husbandry and nutrition hamsters are subject to few health problems and very few diseases. This is one of the many reasons they make such good pets. Disease prevention (or to be more accurate, "wellness") isn't difficult, and it isn't expensive.

Prevention heads off problems before they can start. Start by finding a veterinarian who knows about hamsters (not all of them do, and you need someone who is not only nearby but good). Call a couple of local animal hospitals and ask which of their veterinarians is good with hamsters (or ask the veterinarian you use for your other pets if he or she is comfortable with hamsters). Ask your local pet store which veterinarian they use for their hamsters. If you have been talking to a breeder about buying a hamster, ask him or her for a recommendation. Go online and check local networks for any suggestions; Angie's List can be a very useful resource. Keep the information you collect handy; with any sort of luck you won't need it. But when faced with the prospect of the teary-eyed face of your child because "Teddy" isn't eating, you'll be glad you have the info.

Prevention starts with a good diet. This avoids weakened bones or any of a host of vitamin-deficiency diseases. A good commercial hamster food is your best defense against illness of any sort. But not all commercial hamster foods are created equal. Some hamsters may gobble up brand A of hamster diet; others may dig through brand B diet with the "there has to be something better farther down!" attitude. This is where you're better off with an everything-is-the-same kibble diet as opposed to a seed mix. Think of it as a dish of mixed nuts—no one actually grabs a handful—they oh so casually pick out the nuts they like the best. Hamsters are just like people in this respect; they'll gobble down the fat-rich calcium-miserly sunflower seeds and wait expectantly for a new serving.

Do stay tuned into what's happening in the world of pet food. You may remember a problem with melamine being found in dog treats a few years ago, and some kind of serious problem with dog jerky treats more recently. These sorts of errors don't happen frequently, but they do happen, especially when regulations are lax or enforcement is spotty. You may be more comfortable buying a hamster

kibble that is made in a country where manufacturing plants are inspected.

Your hamster always needs a ready supply of clean drinking water.

Don't keep your pet in a damp, enclosed area; hamsters evolved in deserts and grassy plains, and they are adapted to low humidity levels. Remember that your hamster generates some moisture with his by-products and that damp cages smell a lot more than dry cages. Change the substrate and bedding at least weekly.

Hamsters, even those social species, need hiding places. This gives each individual hamster a way to avoid the stress of dealing with life in a cage. For those few types that can live together, put multiple sleeping boxes or the tubes from paper towels in the cage, to offer privacy to those that might need it. A few pieces of paper toweling or toilet paper squares will give them the distraction of fluffing up the bedding.

You already know about the benefits of exercise for humans. Hamsters are no exception. An exercise wheel gives them a chance to exercise regularly and to relieve stress. If the cage is too small for an exercise wheel, get a bigger cage—experiments have shown hamsters that are moved from small cages to larger cages spend less time in their exercise wheel (but they still use it).

Avoid falls always. When you handle your hamster, hang on to him so he can't wiggle out of your hands and dive like a fur-covered sausage to the floor

Rate Yourself on Prevention

Give yourself five points for every question you can answer "Yes."

	Yes	No
Is my hamster's diet the best I can find, and is the protein content about 15 percent or higher?	___	___
Is the food fresh?	___	___
Is the drinking water always clean, and can everyone in the cage reach the drinking tube?	___	___
Do I clean the cage every week and change the bedding as well?	___	___
Is the caging located in an area that isn't too damp, and is the hamster cage located where the hamster has a chance to look out at the world around him?	___	___
Do I hold my hamster enough so he isn't frightened of me, and do I give him a brief health inspection every week or so?	___	___
Have I inspected my hamster for lumps and bumps, and have I inspected his mouth for even teeth wear?	___	___
Do I provide safe chew toys and an exercise wheel for my hamster?	___	___
Have I made sure the cage is securely closed and have I inspected the cage regularly for sharp edges?	___	___

Evaluation: 30–35 points: You know what you're doing.

20–25 points: You need to work harder at hamster caretaking.

Under 20 points: Maybe you don't really want a hamster.

below. (Holding your hamster in any of the three hamster holds also prevents damage to you when your hamster tries to turn around and give you a good nip.)

Bites from other cage mates can fail to heal and cause abscesses. Caging Syrian or unacquainted dwarf hamsters separately will avoid fighting and damage from bites.

Providing only safe chew toys will avoid stomach blockage when your hamster manages to nibble his way through part of the chew toy.

Detecting Illness

You and your hamster may enjoy every moment of its life together with nary a sniffle. But this dispassionate attitude will fly out the window the day you look in your hamster's cage and he's crouched in a corner with his fur ruffed up and his once bright eyes looking dull. Hamsters are so small, their body reserves are used up quickly. Your sick hamster needs help, or he may die.

Are there any other signs of hamster illness? What was his reaction when you open the cage door? Hamsters that feel good tend to regard the opening of the cage door as a Good Sign, Possibly Meaning Food. Their noses go up in the air, and you can see their whiskers vibrating and the upper lip lifted as they pick up and try to interpret the signs—Worth getting out of bed for? Is it possibly a sunflower seed? Or, gee, it's only That Person again, I'm going back to sleep.

If your hamster has a satin coat, is the fur smooth and sleek? Healthy hamsters have a sleek coat. If you have a rex, when they're ill, their coat seems ruffled and dry looking.

Do your hamster's eyes look bright and alert? A well hamster has shiny eyes, and there's no discharge in the corners of the eyes.

Look at your hamster's nose. His nose should be dry and not runny.

Any change in normal behavior—including a lack of interest in play—may mean illness.

Signs of Illness in a Hamster

- Little or no interest in food
- Loss of weight
- Change in wake/sleep cycle
- Eyes: reddening of the conjunctiva, discharge, adhered eyelids
- Behavior changes: increased aggression, depression, reluctance to move around
- Posture: curled position although hamster is awake, rigid standing, stiff gait
- Appearance: wet tail, diarrhea, loss of hair, scaly skin

Finally, lift your hamster up and check his anal area. Is it dry? A wet anal area, or a hamster sitting in his own feces and not moving to a dry spot in the cage, is the mother of all bad signs. You gotta get him help.

Hamsters that don't feel good tend to tune out the world. Hamsters that are ill generally don't drink water, and they won't eat. They have a "leave me alone" distracted attitude and act briefly nippy if you bother them. They sit hunched over, as if to protect their body. The eyes are dull, teary, and may look sunken—partly due to the disease process and partly due to loss of body moisture or dehydration. You need to do something.

First Actions

What do you do until you figure out what is wrong and either fix it yourself or take your pet to your veterinarian? First of all, if your hamster isn't by himself, separate him from all other hamsters, and all animals, for that matter. Put the cage in an area or niche that's in the 70–85°F (21–29°C) temperature range. If your hamster is in a wire mesh or wire-barred cage, make sure that the room is free from drafts or that you cover one end of the cage to provide a draft-free area. It might even be best if the cage is in a room other than the usual hamster room, if only to remind you when you see the cage that the hamster within needs special tending.

If your hamster has diarrhea and his cage is dirty as a result, clean the cage thoroughly, but disturb him as little as possible while you do this. Wash your hands before you start, and again when you finish. If he's in his sleeping box, you can lift out the sleeping

A hamster that hides continually may be ill or under a great deal of stress (and stressed hamsters quickly become sick hamsters).

Campbell's coats may be smooth, rough (shown here), or long.

box with him inside, put in fresh substrate and bedding, and put the box back in the cage. Be especially careful when you come into contact with a sick hamster's feces. Dried aerosol from feces can literally drift anywhere and can be inhaled by you or any other breathing creature, not a good idea when your hamster is sick. Keep in mind that hamsters practice coprophagy, meaning they are prompted by instinct to consume the soft bowel movement, the cecotropes, when they emerge from the anus. Diarrhea is deadly for them.

If there are any toys or an exercise wheel in the cage, wash them in soapy water, then dunk them in a solution of 10 percent bleach (this is 10 percent by volume, or ¼ cup of bleach to 2¼ cups of water). Then rinse everything well, so there is no detectable odor of bleach (if you can smell it with that great huge insensitive nose of yours, think of what it must smell like to your sick hammie),

let them dry, and put them back in the cage. Take the discarded substrate and bedding material out to your garbage can.

Put in fresh food and fresh water. Wash your hands when you're done, so you won't spread any possible "bug" to other hamsters, other pets, your family, or to yourself.

Talk to Your Veterinarian

Call your veterinarian and talk to her or him about the symptoms you've noticed and how long your hamster has been ill. Ask about the fees, to avoid surprises. Many veterinarians can provide you with information on an interest-free credit card (interest free if you pay it off within 6 months). Your veterinarian doesn't make any money off these cards, but they do provide a

Antibiotics That Will Kill Your Hamster

Hamsters can tolerate many antibiotics, but a few of them will kill good bacteria and leave the wrong kind of bacteria.

Make a copy of this antibiotic list and don't forget it when you take your ill hamster to your veterinarian. Your veterinarian is extremely knowledgeable, but he/she will appreciate this list. You are also extremely bright and would never, ever, dose your hamsters with your own leftover antibiotics.

Here's the Do Not Use list: Penicillin, ampicillin, erythromycin, lincomycin, vancomycin and the cephalosporins. Using these will cause death, preceded by loss of appetite (anoxia) and diarrhea.

his cage, if it's a transportable cage. I used a deep plastic bucket with fresh shavings on the bottom. The bucket was about 18 inches deep, so I wasn't worried about drafts or my hamster leaping out. If you're going out in cold weather, you might want to cover the bucket or cage with a towel.

Be prepared to answer questions about your hamster, what species it is, how old it is, what you feed it, how long you've had it, whether there are any new hamsters in your house, and how long your hamster has been sick. He may ask if there have been any stressors or changes in your household, like a newly installed air conditioner, or if any chemicals have been in use around the house (painting your house qualifies as chemical use in this case). Offer to take your hamster out of its cage and hand it to your vet-

The satin coat on a Roborovski may look greasy, but that's just how the coat looks. It does not indicate illness.

way for you to pay your veterinarian and then budget the card payments.

Most veterinarians are very reasonable about charging for pocket pets. Sometimes the problem is so minute that your veterinarian can offer a suggestion over the phone, if she or he has already seen your hamster. But if your veterinarian hasn't seen your hamster before, or if your hamster isn't eating or drinking, you'll need to take your hamster in. If your hammie is sick, and your veterinarian has evening hours, make an appointment in the evening so your hamster will be naturally awake. Transport your hamster in

erinarian. Many animals are territorial about their cages, and veterinarians try to avoid getting bitten. Usually the animals they deal with have more teeth (dogs have 42 vs. 16 for a Syrian, but at that point who's counting?), so be understanding of this reluctance.

Hamster diseases are generally grouped by the causative agent. We'll begin with what I'll call mechanical problems, which are pretty straightforward and easy to correct. The actual healing may take some time, but at least the cause is easy to identify and correct.

Broken bones: Your hamster takes a flying leap off a tabletop and lands heavily. When you pick him up, you notice he won't put any weight on his fore limb, and he seems to be in pain. He may have broken a leg. Put him in his own cage, away from everything else. Take out his wheel and any toys. If you think the leg is broken, talk to your veterinarian about options. Foremost would be pain control; many vet-

erinarians won't splint or place a cast on something as small as a hamster (yes, there are veterinarians who will, but you'll need to find a specialist or exotic veterinarian), and hamsters are pretty good at chewing off any sort of bandage when you're not looking. Your exotic veterinarian is going to be your go-to person for diagnosis for the leg and to make sure nothing else is wrong with your pet. There's nothing you can do for internal bleeding—there's no sort of animal trauma surgery show on TV to spur veterinarians into funding and building trauma centers for animals, and few people want to spend a thousand dollars or so on emergency abdominal surgery for their hamster. The exotic veterinarian who previewed this manuscript noted that healing time for a broken limb is close to six weeks. Talk to your exotic veterinarian to make sure he or she is okay with placing the hamster in a solid-walled cage by him- or herself (take out the exercise wheel), not handling the animal for six weeks, and administering pain control and feeding a good diet with a calcium supplement.

Bites: Hamsters do tend to fight with each other, and bites are part of that scenario. It doesn't seem to matter who starts a fight, or even what sex the combatants are. Because caging isn't big enough for hamsters to escape each other, fighting and the stress of being on guard tends to go on and on, with only short breaks in between. Unless you're right on hand and intervene, there's a winner and a loser.

Roborovski hamsters in particular can be rapidly overwhelmed by an infection.

To inspect your hamster for bite marks, hold him in your hands and run your fingertips gently over his body. You're going to feel for rough spots on the skin, which can be healed bite marks; for swellings; and for tender spots, which can be unhealed wounds. The vast majority of times, bites heal well without any intervention on your part, but if you find an open wound, clean it with soap and water, and rinse the wound well. You can't add a topical antibiotic—hamsters are groomers, and anything you put on their skin, they'll lick off. You may want to talk to your veterinarian about pain medication and/or an oral anti-inflammatory. Most veterinarians will want to see the animal before prescribing any drug.

Abscesses: Sometimes the wound heals over before the infection inside is eliminated. The result is a sealed-off infection called an abscess, a pocket containing damaged tissue and pus (a combination of bacteria and the carcasses of white blood cells that have swallowed up bacteria and died as a result). Abscesses aren't contagious in the usual sense, although the bacteria they contain can certainly cause abscesses in other hamsters if the hamsters have wounds.

Abscesses look like swollen areas on the hamster's body or on its limbs. These areas are also very tender to the touch, due to the pressure they exert on neighboring healthy tissue, the destruction of the tissue within them, and because of the toxins secreted by the bacterial contents.

Some abscesses are actually hard to the touch, which tells you something of the pressure within. Look for redness of the skin over and surrounding the abscess (you can simply blow the fur aside to see the color of the skin—even the lightest touch of your hand will be painful). Your hamster may clearly display concern with the site, scratching it or around it, or endlessly grooming the fur around the site. If the abscess is on the face, expect to see drooling, facial swelling, perhaps bad breath (you'd have to get close to experience this). Lack of appetite, depression/lack of activity, and weight loss are other typical symptoms, and learning of the discomfort abscesses can cause, you can certainly understand *why*.

Your veterinarian will use a syringe and the fine needle to try to aspirate some of the pus from within the abscess. Don't be surprised if some of the pus dribbles out of the puncture wound made by the needle, but most of the contents are too thick to go through a needle prick. He or she may want to use ultrasound or radiograph to determine the size of the abscess. Sometimes the abscess is drained, using a sterile scalpel to create a tiny nick into the abscess. A local or general anesthetic is usually administered to alleviate the pain of the cleaning process—although it may not look like a painful procedure, hamsters can die of shock when "wounded" by humans, without an anesthetic. Hamsters can deal with wounds inflicted by other hamsters far more calmly than wounds inflicted by humans.

After the abscess has been opened and cleaned, an antibiotic is usually injected into the former abscess site, and then administered (probably orally) for a few days afterward, to ensure that the bacteria are eliminated. Once the abscess has been treated, your hamster should regain its appetite and regain any weight lost. Pain medication should be discussed.

Eyes: Hamsters do develop eye problems in response to eye injuries or infections. Some kinds of Campbell's hamsters are born without eyes. Hamsters also develop cataracts. If your hamster keeps his eyes closed, as if they hurt him, put his cage in a darkened area. Change to a different substrate, if you're keeping your hamster on a potential "scratching" substrate like pine shavings. Talk to your veterinarian about your hamster's eye problems; she or he may prescribe drops and perhaps an eye wash to cleanse the area.

Cheek pouch injury: Your hamster's cheek pouches may be bitten in a fight, or your hamster may find a sharp object in his cage and damage his cheek pouches. If your hamster seems unable to empty his cheek pouches, hold him on his back with the nape hold and try to see what the problem is. You may need to get your veterinarian's help to remove foreign objects from your hamster's cheek pouches, but don't delay. Cheek pouches are not immunologically

My Hamster Died and I Don't Know Why

In a worst-case scenario, if your hamster has died and you really want to find out what happened, yes, you can have a necropsy performed. Call your veterinarian, and ask him/her to fix tissue specimens for the necropsy. Put your hamster's body in a cooler, add some ice, and take the cooler to your veterinarian. She or he will take a stool specimen and lung, heart, brains, liver, spleen, and other tissue samples, and immerse them in small bottles of formalin solution. Your veterinarian will also call the necropsy lab and make the necessary shipping arrangements. The lab will fax the necropsy results to your veterinarian, and she/he will call you; this usually takes about a week.

active. This means that the pouches are less capable of fighting off an injury or infection. In addition, a hamster with cheek pouch problems is in all likelihood not eating. Again, discuss pain management with your veterinarian.

Teeth: Hamsters' front incisors are designed to rub against each other when they are nibbling on something, and they are supposed to wear evenly. This doesn't always happen. Hamsters need their front teeth to be perfectly aligned so they can eat. When the teeth don't wear evenly, the unmatched teeth may grow into the roof of the mouth or into the pouches.

To check your hamster's teeth, put your hamster in a nape hold and look at his teeth. If you see that one tooth is longer than its mate, you can use a pair of fingernail clippers to gently trim the offending tooth. Nip off tiny bits at a time until the teeth are aligned. If this is more than you want to take on, your veterinarian can trim your hamster's teeth.

Check the teeth once a month so you can get the problem corrected if it reoccurs.

If the tooth base seems inflamed or the face or gums swollen, take your hamster to your veterinarian. She will extract the infected tooth and prescribe antibiotics and appropriate medications until the gum heals.

Sometimes the cheek teeth are the site of the problem. Unlike rabbits, whose continuously growing cheek teeth may be prone to periodontal disease and abscesses, the hamsters (and mice, rats, and gerbils) have short-crowned, rooted cheek teeth that are subject to cavities and periodontal disease. Try to avoid sugar-laden treats and snacks. Your veterinarian can help by tooth extraction and antibiotics, but this is a largely avoidable problem and an expense few owners are willing to incur.

Ears: Hamsters do develop ear problems. Symptoms are holding the head tilted to one side, shaking the head, and scratching the ear area with the foot. You won't be able to see inside your hamster's ear without an otoscope, so you'll need to see your

Check your hamster's teeth for uneven wear.

veterinarian for assistance on a possible ear problem. If you want to ease the itching overnight, mix a teaspoon each of water and white vinegar and put a drop into the hamster's ear. Let him shake out what he can. If the itching doesn't stop, see your veterinarian.

Heat Stroke: Although hamsters are desert animals, they burrow to avoid the heat. Some burrows are 8 feet deep; for hamsters in the desert, heat isn't a problem. When your hamster's cage is near a sunny window, in your car, or in an unventilated room, he can't avoid the heat. He may cope by breathing heavily and may lie on his belly to expose more of his body for cooling off. He may become semiconscious. Your hamster will die very quickly, and in distress, unless you take steps immediately. Move the cage to a cool spot, take the hamster out, and run cool (not cold) water over his body until he is alert and the high breathing rate has slowed. Dry him off

Male long-haired Syrians can develop an amazing coat.

gently, and put him in his clean, dry cage away from any heat to rest. The cage should have fresh water available. Use a plastic eyedropper to offer your hamster water or Pedialyte, the balanced electrolyte solution available in your grocery store's baby food area, and take him to your veterinarian. There's far more going on in your hamster's body, due to heat prostration, than you can deal with at home.

Respiratory Problems

Hamsters that have difficulty breathing may be responding to fine dust or ammonia fumes of dirty substrate in their caging, or aromatic oils if pine or cedar shavings have been used. Bac-terial pneumonia or, rarely, viral pneumonia caused by a virus called Sendai also occur.

Watch for signs of labored breathing, often accompanied by discharge from the nose and eyes, loss of appetite, and weight loss. Check the caging conditions. Has any construction occurred in your house? That fine plaster dust is deadly to hamsters. Clean his cage, and ask a friend to take care of him until all the construction is done and all the painting is done. If the substrate could be the problem, change substrate. If you think your hamster is allergic to wood fiber or even the smell of the wood shavings/pellets, use the wheat grass or the hibiscus pellets. Has your hamster's cage bedding been dampened and you didn't catch the problem quickly? Pneumonia develops when the hamster's resistance is challenged by damp caging and bedding, or when he is stressed by protracted drafts with no way to avoid them.

In a creature as small as a hamster, pneumonia causes big-time heart distress. Not only does your hamster have trouble absorbing enough oxygen across the surface of his lungs, but his heart works harder to push blood through the inflamed lungs. Heart failure or a blood clot thrown into the lungs is often the fatal result. Your hamster is probably too sick to get well on his own. Take your hamster to your veterinarian. He or she will prescribe an antibiotic (probably administered via water bottle).

Sendai disease, caused by a virus called *Paramyxovirus,* is a highly contagious virus that is deadly to hamster colonies. It is also causes high mortality in mice and rats, so if you're also the owner of a pet rat or mouse, you have double cause for concern. Keep your pet away from other hamsters and, of course, away from your other pet rodents.

Cancer

When you find a lump or an open area on your hamster's body, your first thought may be that it is cancer. If the area is actually two spots, one above each hip, relax. You've found your hamster's flank glands, a very normal part of hamster bodywork.

The other good news here is that the cancer rate in hamsters is among the lowest in all the pet rodents, and it is usually associated with advanced age. External tumors are usually diagnosed/recognized long before internal tumors are suspected, and the external tumors may be removed successfully. If the tumor is internal, symptoms are usually limited to weight loss and general lethargy in the hamster. One day your hamster will go to sleep and not wake up, and unless you have an autopsy done, you won't know if the cancer or old age killed him.

Gastrointestinal Problems

Enteropathies—diseases of the gut—are very common in pet hamsters. The diseases are spread by direct fecal-oral contact (kind of hard to avoid in a creature that consumes its own cecotropes) and fomite contamination (a fomite is anything emitted or shed by a sick person or creature, like mucous sprays from sneezing, saliva, feces, urine, vomit). Better husbandry and better medical treatment has turned these often-fatal infections from "too bad, he's dead" to "he really can get better."

Perhaps the most common is "wet-tail," most commonly caused by the bacteria *Lawsonia intracellularis*. This is the bacterial disease that badly affected hamster keeping in the 1950s. Wet-tail is used as a generic term for any type of diarrhea so acute the hamster cannot keep himself clean. His rump is wet from the unending diarrhea, the soft, mucousy feces are on his feet, on the floor of the cage, in his bedding, and if you hold him, on your hands. The odor is pungent. Not only is your hamster uncomfortable, he may be too sick to care. It is highly contagious from hamster to hamster and particularly hard on hamsters less than twelve weeks old. Be sure to wash your hands, before and after you handle him; you don't want to add to his bacterial load from your not-so-clean hands, and you don't want any of his bacteria on your hands.

Symptoms in addition to the stained tail and diarrhea include lethargy, failure to eat or drink, irritability, and ruffled hair. Unless relief is quickly given, the colon may telescope into itself (intussception) or protrude out the rectum (called a rectal prolapse). Prognosis for a young hamster is very poor even with early detection. The prognosis for an adult hamster is better. Treatment is usually with antibiotics; most pet stores stock an antibiotic medication for wet-tail, but you might prefer to get medication from your veterinarian. She or he can identify the type of bacteria from a fecal smear and will know which medication to prescribe, and *how much* to prescribe (this makes a difference—you would not adminsiter the same dose to a Campbell's as you would to a Syrian due to their size/weight difference). Although most commonly caused by *Lawsonia intracellularis*, other bacteria, such as *E. coli*, can also be the culprit.

Another type of acute diarrhea is called antibiotic-associated enterotoxaemia. Normally, your hamster's gut has a variety of microorganisms, all living more or less at peace with one another. But when that balance is altered by antibiotics, the mood "down there" can shift, with big changes in power ensuing. Pathogenic organisms bloom. At least three kinds of clostridial bacteria can be found in most hamster guts, and it's not the bacteria themselves that kill the hamster, but the toxins the anaerobic bacteria secrete as part of their normal day-to-day living. (Anaerobic bacteria are bacteria that live quite well without air. These are the bacteria that make a poorly sealed can of green beans swell and the ends of the can bulge out. As a group the anaerobics are unfriendly bacteria.)

Symptoms begin six to forty eight hours after the antibiotics have been administered. They include diarrhea, swelling, and internal bleeding. The unfriendly bacteria get a toe-hold, so to speak, in your hamster's gut when your hamster has been weakened by another disease and/or when it has been on prolonged antibiotic therapy. The normal gut flora has been thrown into imbalance by the antibiotics or a poor diet.

Talk to your veterinarian about what needs to be done. Treatment and control come through dealing with the stressing agency (Is the hamster cage next to your pet skunk's bed? Move the cage to another room, high up on a table!) and helping the friendly gut

Hamsters gnaw on their cage bars when they are stressed or bored. You need to discover the reason and fix it.

bacteria to become reestablished. Some people administer droplets of yogurt with an eyedropper in an effort to reestablish the intestinal flora; others feed their hamster the stool of another, healthy hamster (the process is called transfaunation, although transfloration would seem to be more accurate).

Tip: if your hamster is ill and refuses to feed, you can try feeding vegetable baby foods via an eyedropper. Don't try to administer more than a quarter-teaspoon—remember your hamster's stomach is small. You can also try to administer yogurt; the flavored varieties may be accepted more readily, and

their higher sugar content may give your hamster a boost.

Salmonellosis

Salmonella bacteria are found almost anywhere. Salmonella is ubiquitous in soil. Humans can get it from preparing eggs. (The bacteria are on the outside of the eggshell. The egg is broken into a bowl or into a frying pan. The human, who has handled the egg, goes on to prepare the eggs for a meal and just doesn't wash his or her hands after cracking the egg. The egg is cooked and ready to eat and somehow the human touches it as it goes onto the plate. Salmonella is transferred from the human's hand to the surface of the cooked egg, which has cooled down enough so the bacteria aren't killed. The human eats the egg and comes down with a case of salmonellosis a day or two later.) Salmonella bacteria can affect hamsters as well as humans, and hamsters generally get the disease the same way we do: they eat infected food. You can avoid this by washing the fruits and vegetables you give your hamsters, the same way you would if you were going to eat them, and washing your own hands before you handle your hamster.

There may be no observable symptoms of salmonellosis. The infection overwhelms your hamster, and he or she dies. Salmonellosis may also cause your hamster to act just a bit "off" and lose weight over a period of a few weeks. Your veterinarian will culture a stool specimen. Treatment may be with an antibiotic (see the caution on antibiotic use, page 103) or you and your veterinarian may decide that euthanization is the better answer.

Fungus and Parasites

Ringworm

We live more closely allied with fungus than many of us would like to admit. Humans get athlete's foot, which is caused by a fungus. The fungi that cause ringworm find homes in dogs, rabbits, humans, and hamsters. Hamsters that get ringworm have generally been made susceptible by damp, dirty, or stressful housing and fed inadequate diets. Symptoms of ringworm in hamsters are scaling skin, hair loss, and itching, much the same symptoms as mites. Your veterinarian will need to make the diagnosis and provide treatment.

Mites

If your hamster is losing his hair, has scaling skin or dry, scaly, scabby inflamed skin, a rough coat, and tends to scratch himself a lot, he may have mites. Although mites are rare in domestic hamsters, they do occur, and they are bad news. It isn't just that your hamster has blood-sucking tiny mites living in his skin (that's why he's so

Expect to find that your hamster spends his time watching you.

itchy and uncomfortable), but hamsters don't contract mites unless there's something else wrong. Hamsters have to be both susceptible to mites and exposed to them to contract them. Diagnosis for mites is made initially by appearance of the hamster's skin and coat, and confirmed by a microscopic examination of a skin scraping. Mites are compact little eight-legged insect relatives, and when they are disturbed, as when taken from the soft juicy skin where they've set up housekeeping, they wave their fat, stubby, bristly legs around and move their mouthparts as if in silent protest. Treatment may be via oral or injected Ivermectin. Avoid reinfestation by a thorough cleaning of the cage after each injection.

is an older hamster with abdominal swelling who looks uncomfortable and isn't eating, talk to your veterinarian about euthanization. Allowing a pet to remain in pain, with no relief until it dies, should be avoided.

Campbell's blacks will "silver" with age.

When Your Hamster Gets Old

Hamsters rarely live more than 2–2½ years, and the signs of aging are pretty clear. In addition to general thinning of hair, general slowness of reactions, lethargy, and decreased appetite, some strains of hamsters are very susceptible to liver cysts. These cysts can be very large and cause the abdomen to bulge out. Liver failure with the resulting cirrhosis and amyloidosis (deposits of amyloids, a white protein substance, in all body organs) are common problems in hamsters over a year old.

If you are worried about your hamster being in pain as it ages, or if it

Inherited Problems

Syrian hamsters are prone to a hereditary cardiomyopathy (heart failure) that produces clinical signs of heart failure when the hamster is as young as six months of age. Symptoms include lethargy, labored breathing, perhaps edema or swelling, and cold extremities—pretty much the same symptoms as a human in heart failure. Diagnosis is based on clinical signs and radiographs (if you're willing to pay for these), which tells you that you have not only a very sick hamster but a very expensive one as well. Your veterinarian may want to start treatment, using much the same medications used to treat human heart failure. You may opt for euthanization.

Chapter Nine
Hamster Clubs and Showing Your Hamster

The Clubs

Hamster clubs were begun first in England, to promote Syrian hamsters as pets. The first club was formed in 1945, a few years after the first laboratory hamsters were smuggled into the country. Like dog and rabbit clubs, the membership soon progressed from mutual admiration and sales/exchanges to actual competitions where hamsters were rated on their size, shape, and color/coat. Categories increased to include other hamster breeds. Selective breeding of those early winners brought us the short noses and compact ("cobby" if you're in England) bodies we see on today's Syrians. That's why the Syrians you see in pet stores don't look like the long-bodied creatures a few people may remember from the 1950s.

Selective breeding has brought us a wealth of hamster colors and coat variations, with show standards and names for each. The show standards are steady, quantitative measuring tools, and you can be assured that your Black-eyed Cream will be compared to other Black-eyed Creams.

(Pet stores' names for color varieties are something else, based partially on description and partially on marketing hutzpah.)

Today there are three regional hamster clubs in England, all affiliated with the National Hamster Council (hamsters-uk.org). In the United States, at this time there is just one club, the California Hamster Club.

All of these clubs have Web pages and provide information on hamster keeping and hamster breeding. Some sponsor shows, either by themselves or as a cooperative effort with a guinea pig or rat fancy group (the term "fancy" here only means "to like," as in "I quite fancy chocolate chip cookies").

Hamster clubs do not always list a physical address on their online site. This of course allows everyone their privacy unless they wish it otherwise. Clubs have several categories of membership, based on one's age and how close one might live to the club headquarters' city or to an affiliate club. All can arrange for international memberships and would welcome your membership.

A Campbell's blue cream. The blue color is the result of the black and opal genes.

You may find other clubs, both national and international, listed on the World Wide Web, but hamster clubs tend to be a bit ephemeral. Be a prudent purchaser. If you are interested in joining a hamster club, make contact with a club representative either by phone, e-mail, or letter, before you send in your membership dues.

Hamster Clubs

In the United States:

California Hamster Association
23651 Dune Mear
Lake Forest, CA 92630
chahamsters.org

In the United Kingdom the clubs are affiliated with the National Hamster Council, which is the oldest hamster club anywhere. (Sadly, the British Hamster Association has ceased to exist.)

The Midland Hamster Club
Secretary, Mrs. Sue Carter
24 Shepherds Rise
Vernham Dean, Andover
Hampshire, SP11 0HD
Telephone: 01264 737414
www.midlandhamsterclub.co.uk

The Northern Hamster Club
Secretary, Pat Richardson
7 Main Avenue, Heworth
York YO3 0RT
Phone: 01904 413426
www.northernhamsterclub.co.uk

The Southern Hamster Club
Secretary, Wendy Barry
Phone: 01373 300766
www.southernhamsterclub.co.uk/new

Virtual clubs (online only)
Internet Hamster Association
   of North America
www.ihana.us/clubs.html

The Hamster Club
www.hamster-club.com

Singapore Hamster Club
www.sghamsters.com

The Shows

Hamster shows are for both the hobbyist and for the serious breeder/competitor. Although you may enjoy your hamsters, there are people who take hamster keeping and showing very seriously (some people won't enter a competition when they don't like the judges at the show). But the majority of the hobbyists at shows are there because they enjoy it.

Shows exist to promote hamster keeping, and hamster sales/trades are part of every show. They offer you a way to buy or trade for a hamster you probably would never see elsewhere. Who could resist the chance to add a charmer like a black-eyed cream or a sable roan to one's hamster family?

Shows may be either fun shows, or a combination of fun and conformation/color shows. The fun competition usually has a category for first-time contestants, judging on your pet's condition and tameness. There are also ribbons or prizes for the best pet, the biggest, the most spirited, the oddest color combination, and the "most alike" hamster pairs. The categories are a bit quirky and apt to change from year to year.

The conformation competition is separated into Syrian and Dwarf groups; the Dwarf groups include the lesser-known and not quite as popular Roborovski and Chinese hamsters. The conformation shows in England use the standards set by the British Hamster Association, and those standards are quite exact.

Each show entry requires a fee, which may be less for club members. Most clubs firmly request preregistration for a conformation competition.

Show qualifications also include ages (typically, Syrians must be five weeks old while Dwarves must be four weeks old). The cooperative shows, shows that cater to mixed species like the fancy rat/mouse and hamster shows, ask that you quarantine your show animals for a month before the show. This means you agree to "isolate" your show animals for that time and that you will not allow any births to occur within the quarantined group, nor will you bring any new purchases into the group. Quarantine helps to avoid the spread of communicable diseases like wet-tail or the Sendai virus. The possibility of contracting communicable disease puts fear into the heart of every hamster fancier; unless this fear is allayed, many breeders won't exhibit their best stock at a show, which makes a show pretty pointless for the competition.

Each animal, whether entered in the fun or conformation category, must

A cream Campbell's with ruby eyes.

Hamster Classes for Conformation: Syrians

Type (body shape)	25 points
Color	30 points
Fur	20 points
Size	10 points
Condition	10 points
Eyes and ears	5 points

Color groups:

Agouti (fur is actually banded—dark at the base, light in the middle, and dark tip)	Silver Gray	Black-eyed Cream
	Honey	Red-eyed Cream
	Lilac	Black-eyed Ivory
	Rust	Red-eyed Ivory
Beige	Smoke Pearl	Sable
Blonde	Yellow	Dark-eared White
Cinnamon	Self (fur is one color)	Flesh-eared White
Golden	Black	Black-eared White
Dark Gray	Chocolate	
Light Gray	Copper	

Patterned varieties:

Dominant Spot	Roan	Tortoiseshell and White
White Banded	Tortoiseshell	Dominant Spot Banded

Coats:

Long-haired	Satin	Rex

be by him/herself in a wire or plastic container. The small to medium Pen Pal terrariums are typical show cages. Some hamster organizations have show cages you can rent for the show's duration.

Each cage top must bear a label that lists the competition, not the owner's name. Each cage must be stocked with clean bedding, food, and a water source. The water source can be fresh fruit like grapes or apple slices.

You'll be asked to check in about an hour before the show's formal opening time. This will give you enough time to pick up your paperwork at the registration table, to have your entries checked by the attending veterinarian (this last item isn't always a necessity), and to put your cages on the correct tables.

The first chocolate hamsters were "self" — a solid color. In competition, anything other than white feet would be a disqualification.

The time between check-in and the actual show gives you a chance to visit the vendors. The hamsters that are offered for sale may be placed on a separate table, near the dry goods. Not only will there be imprinted key chains, mugs, mouse pads, T-shirts, and caging and cage accessories beyond your wildest dreams, but you'll have a chance to buy foodstuffs or shavings, often for less than you'd pay at your local pet store. And if you pick up an extra hamster here or a trio there, it's because you've gotten a terrific deal on a line you may never see anywhere else. What an efficient use of your time!

Judging

Judging only takes a few minutes per hamster because the judges really do know what they are looking for. The judges will open your cage, pick up your hamster, examine its coat, feet, face, and body shape. Good behavior on the part of the hamster is important; most judges penalize a biting hamster one point. Winners are awarded ribbons with rosettes and loving cups, sometimes large enough for the hamster to sleep in.

In conformation shows, the BHA standard is the best, but it isn't used for all shows. There aren't many formally trained judges in the States who know and use the BHA standard. Training consists of four stages: book steward, pen steward, junior judge, and finally, senior judge, and it isn't easy to get in the United States. You can train over the Internet with senior judges who are in England, but a portion of it is has to be onsite in England.

Useful Addresses and Literature

Just so you'll know—many hamster sites are based in England, because the interest in hamsters is far greater there than in the United States.

Web Sites
The Complete Hamster Site
www.hamsters.co.uk

Hamster info
netvet.wustl.edu/

California Hamster Association
32651 Dune Mear
Lake Forest, CA 92630
www.chahamsters.org

National Hamster Council
hamsters-uk.org

Internet Hamster Association of North America
www.ihana.us/clubs.html

American Fancy Rat and Mouse Association
www.AFRMA.org

Association for Exotic Mammal Veterinarians
aemv.org

Petfinder.com for hamster adoption

Remember to make sure any organization is currently active before you send in any donation or membership payment.

Books
Fritzsche, Peter. *My Hamster.* Hauppauge NY: Barrons Educational Series, 2007.

Hill, Lorraine. *Hamsters A to Z.* Neptune City, NJ: TFH, 2001.

Keeling, C.H. *Dwarf Hamsters.* Plymouth, Devon: Basset Publications, 1987.

Logsdail, Chris and Logsdail, Peter. *Hamster Lopedia,* Dorking, Surrey: RingPress, a division of Interpet Publishing, 2002.

Marsh, Albert F. *The Hamster Manual.* St. Petersburg, FL: Gulf Hamstery, 1952.

Siegel, Harold, editor, *The Hamster: Reproduction and Behavior.* New York, NY: Plenum Press, 1985.

Vanderlip, Sharon, DVM. *Dwarf Hamsters* Hauppauge, NY: Barron's Educational Series, 1999.

von Frisch, Otto. *Hamsters.* Hauppauge, NY: Barron's Educational Series, 1997.

Index